THE FAMILY MONEY GAME

...YOU CAN WIN IT!

by Robert Steen

Published by Bookmakers Guild, Inc., Longmont, Colorado

Contents

Tables

My Uncle Lewis coached the best baseball team in the South. His team never lost a game. I asked him once how he managed it—never losing. He spit out his chewing tobacco, traced a small baseball diamond in the dirt with his foot, and said:

"I jest told them boys they weren't playin' baseball, they wus playing' hardball."

I never really understood these inspiring words. I mention them here because the publisher gave me this space. I'd like to use it to ask Uncle Lewis what in tarnation he meant.

Introduction

I don't want to dwell on my credentials for writing this book—the tree nursery that tried to change our front lawn into a forest or the finance companies represented on my wife's side at the wedding. Let's just say that when it comes to managing the family's finances, I've had experience in the trenches. Forget about the bargain lawn mower that wouldn't cut butter, much less grass. And never mind about the stock I bought at ten dollars a share and sold for ten cents. What matters is that I have long since reached the last straw: that moment when each of us decides to do a better job of managing our money.

Of course, we all have different "last straws." Maybe it is the old washing machine that finally quits and somehow manages to flood the basement as a parting shot. Or it might be the two month's worth of salary the government claims you owe as back taxes. Whatever your last straw is, if it has you gritting your teeth to do something about your family's finances, you have taken a step toward a better money management. Hopefully, this book will assist you in the rest of the journey.

Tax-deferred equipment leases, zero coupon bonds, oil income partnerships, and no-load mutual funds are a few of the things that you won't read about in this book. Sadly, information on hoarding gold has also been omitted. Today, financial supermarkets can transfer funds, sell a deferred annuity, or charge a pair of jeans to your account—all in the same store. Moreover, a brokerage firm can set up an asset management account to insure that every penny of your money is properly invested to assist in paying for all of this convenience. With this kind of sophistication, you are probably rolling in the money. If not, maybe you don't need more sophistication.

If the truth were known, few families lose the money game because they don't understand modern financial instruments. Instead, they lose because they don't follow the money basics. You don't have to be a financial genius to win the money game. But you must know why you play and what is required to win.

Regrettably, there are some things this book won't do. You should know that it won't make you rich. Nor will it necessarily save your family big dollars while shopping. If you prefer to save the $3.29 for creme rinse and pour used motor oil on your head, feel free to do so. This is a how-to book: how to manage your money better. Think of it as a training exercise for when you *really* strike it rich and need to know how to handle your wealth.

Robert Steen

1

The Game And Why You Are In It

Pay no attention to family finances for a while and watch what happens. They will sink every time. This marvel is probably the work of some ancient law scribbled on a caveman's wall just before he was carted off for not paying his bills. But you don't have to take his word for it. Test it for yourself. Forget about the balance in your checkbook. And don't bother keeping track of the checks written on your account. If you have stocks, ignore any frantic phone calls from your broker. You will soon discover that finances, left to themselves, will go down, never up.

In the old days people took a dim view of being inattentive to money; which usually meant more than a few days in jail plus the spectacle of having your goods repossessed while the neighbors looked on. Now, in our modern age of plastic and electronic finance, anyone can keep up appearances while they sink. The idea here is to let everyone think you are prospering handsomely.

Take my friend, Pete, for example. A few years ago, he took the plunge, as financial people sometimes say. When it was over, he was flat broke. Oddly enough, those of us who watched this amazing feat never saw a thing. Pete always seemed to have plenty of money. If you had lunch with him, he would pay the tab and tip the waiter with a little pile of bills that would choke a horse. His home was in the best neighborhood, his sports car was a sleek, expensive model, and Pete had a membership in the finest country club in town. From all outward appearances, he had it made. But things were not as they seemed. Pete's job and the income it provided could not support his lifestyle. Eventually, his carefree spending and casual attitude toward money matters caught up with him. When the end finally came, it was abrupt. He lost his house and sports car almost overnight, and the country club revoked his membership one day before he could tee off on the first hole.

For wealthy people, this downward trip resembles an overweight duck in a spiral dive. For the rest of us, the view is less spectacular and the crash leaves a smaller crater. Naturally, the thing to remember is to smile nonchalantly on the way down for appearances sake.

Not that being inattentive to money will make you sink all at once. Seldom does it happen this way. More often, the decline is gradual, hardly noticeable at first. But unless action is taken to correct this downfall, speed increases with the descent. And there comes a time when the financial point of no return is reached. This is when you will want to pull the buzzer, as if on the bus to disaster, and get off at the next stop. Unfortunately, the next stop is the bottom. And rich or poor, hitting bottom still exacts the same amount of pain.

This is one compelling reason for paying attention to family finances. It is also why people worry a lot. You should know that with enough worry, the element of surprise can be avoided; you won't be amazed when you hit bottom. So much for worrying. The worst part is that worrying takes considerable energy, the kind that might be put to better use by doing something to avoid financial downfall. But then, why am I telling you this? You already know how much good worrying does and no doubt gave it up for a New Year's resolution. If not, figure that a little concern goes a long way. You must take charge of managing family finances to steer clear of the nose-dive trip.

This is thrilling news, especially if you are the type who is inspired by knowing that your forefathers did a better job of handling their money than you do. Most of us can do without the reminder. Even so, we have all heard at one time or another that we ought to manage our money better. Usually, a friend or relative waits until we have made a money mistake to impart this wisdom. But even if you have heard this adage before, and most of us have, you should have a more sound reason for managing money than simply knowing that your great–grandfather or George Washington thought it a good idea. Moreover, conventional wisdom aside, the nose-dive trip is not why it should be managed. Resolving to manage money for this reason is like taking medicine to avoid the plague. It works, but it is not much fun. Since handling family finances ranks somewhere below taking out the garbage as one of America's favorite pastimes, you owe it to yourself to find a better reason. Otherwise, your interest will wane and your days as chief money manager will be over before they begin.

What our ancestors forgot to mention, and what the caveman never had time to write, was the best reason for managing money. If they had gotten around to it, we might all be the wealthier for it now. Still, these old wisdoms are never lost. They linger on, just waiting to be rediscovered. As it happens, you can find the best reason right here. By writing it on the wall or in some other obvious place, you will always have a handy reminder, and you may also receive credit later when a future generation comes along to unearth this wisdom once again. Here it is: *The best reason for managing money is to get the things you want.* After all, those megabucks are for your benefit—or should be. Can you think of a more worthy cause than your own family's wants? Before you start counting causes like saving the starving chickens in Georgia or preserving the double-beaked, humped-back mosquito, remember that by donating to these or any other favorite causes, you are doing so by choice—which comes back to the original goal of getting the things you want.

Since few people play the money game for the exercise, you may want to try all those ways to get rich that everyone talks about. Earn five hundred a week in your spare time. Or try this: stay within earshot when some investor is about to reveal what his broker knows. If it turns out that his broker doesn't know very much, find another investor. And carry a sack lunch. You can never be certain of how long it might take to overhear investment advice that is worth repeating. In the meantime, read the magazine ads. You could be passing up huge profits in raising earthworms, not to mention the advantages of having your own fishing bait. And you might as well know that others are making a fortune sending out junk mail to people like you and me. Of course, if these methods don't work, simply settle down to earning money with absolutely no investment or risk. How? Know the "secret." Then you can dazzle everyone with your money feats. And while rolling your wheelbarrow of cash to the bank, you will still be missing the real secret for securing your family's wants.

Naturally, if this secret is true to form, it is probably out there in some distant jungle where the natives guard it religiously. But don't pack your bags. You should have a nagging suspicion that this secret

is less exotic and closer to home. In fact, it's so well hidden that few of us recognize it even when we see it. Your neighbor, unwitting lucky soul that he probably is, may have this secret, although he will never admit it. Even if he did, this is not the sort of secret that can be borrowed. You must discover it for yourself. Money won't buy it. And it is a cinch you can't bribe the natives. So what is it? What is this secret for getting your wants from your finances?

A Family Budget!

Granted, budgets are about as popular as root canal work or clogged drain pipes. Tell a friend your family is going on a budget and you will receive the same sympathy as if you'd been hit by a truck. Why all the glamour? Because most people tend to view budgeting as forced penny-pinching. It isn't. Budgeting is planning. It is taking stock of family goals and developing a plan to reach them. If you play the odds, the chances of reaching family goals are greatly improved with a plan. Without one, the odds of a dream home, vacation, or place in the sun suddenly appearing are in the realm of a long shot— about as likely as bank errors in your favor.

Yes, well, you really had in mind something a little more exotic, right? After all, any secret that's worth its mystique is going to have some magic to it. And this one does. If you make a budget too restrictive, it becomes a straitjacket or a ball and chain. Or even worse, a millstone around your neck. What's more, after this strangling transformation, your budget never works again. That's the end of the magic. Unless you count black magic, the kind of hocus-pocus that people least expect to come their way, as one young couple quickly discovered.

Fred and Sally argued about money constantly. Their marriage had begun happily, even joyously, but it had deteriorated into an ongoing battle over money matters. Fred accused Sally of spending too much and wasting money on things they didn't need. Sally accused Fred of being a cheapskate except where his freeloading friends were concerned. Finally weary from arguing, the two resolved to go on a budget and to keep track of every dollar. Each month they agreed to pay all of their bills first and to split the remaining money equally between them. Then in a moment of lesser brilliance, they added one last and regrettable rule: each would decide how the other's share of the remaining dollars should be spent. Surprisingly enough, Fred and Sally stuck with their budget for six weeks. They might have continued with it even longer if Sally had not attacked her spouse for refusing to change a flat tire—a "serious oversight" brought on by six weeks of living with this budget. Luckily, they recognized their problem, deep-sixed their budget, and went to a counsellor. Today, Fred and Sally managed their money with less stringent requirements, though they still use a budget. Even more impressive, they seldom argue anymore. Admittedly, some of the credit for this harmony probably goes to Fred's uncanny ability to change a flat tire in thirty seconds these days.

Even so, black magic is nothing to fool around with. Countless families are broken up each year arguing over money problems. How many of them add to their difficulties by attempting to budget too rigidly, we don't know. But one thing is certain. Fred and Sally were not the first couple to discover black magic. If a budget requires undue sacrifices from your family, sooner or later you will find it in the garbage.

Still, magic is magic. And one little trick brings out the wizards who will swear that budgets can somehow bail people out of a financial mess. The truth is, they won't. Don't count on any magical powers of a budget to bail you out of a financial dilemma. A budget is a management tool and like any other tool, it works only when *you* make it work. It is possible to be extracted from a money mess with the aid of a budget. But *you* do the extracting; the budget is merely along for the ride. With something less than magic, a budget can organize family finances and present information for decision-making. If you use it wisely, take all the credit. If you make lousy decisions, by all means, blame the budget—while you sink.

Okay. So you will manage your family's money very carefully. And you will use a budget, even though you are not thrilled about the idea and instead would prefer something a little more exotic, like the natives in grass skirts. But never mind them. You intend to get your family's wants, if it is the last thing you ever do. As luck would have it, there are people in the world of credit just waiting to help you get them. This is why I mention some of the hazards, like the *Boomerang Game.*

This is the game where people merrily spend money with the aid of easy credit and hope to react fast enough when the bills come due. Credit cards are great for this game. Before the gloss is worn off a new

SPENDING

credit card, you can spend several times the amount of money in your bank account. And the payment isn't due until next month. Even more amazing, you need only to pay the minimum amount due when the statement arrives. This keeps cash available for other purchasing, while you, last of the big spenders, still enjoy your credit card clout. While you bask in the glow of this fun, the financial boomerang is returning on a course aimed directly at you. The first hint it is headed your way is when a merchant accepts a card and comes back saying your credit limit has been exceeded. Players who think quickly, will pull out another credit card. Another sign of trouble is when you can't pay the minimum amounts due on card statements at the end of the month. So much for quick thinking. Since the interest charges usually increase the minimum amount due each month, there is little doubt about the direction the boomerang is headed. A guided missile was never more accurate. Soon everything blows up. The same friendly folks who provided your stake in this game now send nasty letters demanding payment. Your credit rating tumbles to the lowest level—credit addict. In turn, this results in no more credit at a time when it is sorely needed. This game ends when the player can no longer duck the financial boomerang.

A similar version is the *Rebound Game,* where excessive debts have players bouncing from one crisis to another. Credit cards are not needed to play this game. Just borrow from several different sources, including your mother-in-law, to finance the stereo, the new car, the boat, and a trip to the Riviera. Since the money is borrowed from various lenders, no one knows exactly how much debt you are carrying. When running short of cash to make payments, simply rotate who gets paid and who doesn't. This is known as robbing Peter to pay Paul, so to speak. Of course, once Peter is robbed too many times and too frequently, life in the debtor's fast lane begins. It's also about the same time that everyone except your mother-in-law files suit to collect their money. And you can never be too sure about your mother-in-law. This game ends when the player can no longer move at the speed of light to cover all the crises.

If you have been playing either of these games, a budget can help sidestep the melodrama. True, it won't solve every type of crisis, but it can smooth out the ups and downs on the financial side of life. Besides, most of us prefer to watch soap operas on television rather than live them in real life.

Not that money can't be managed without a budget. You could be doing fairly well without one. You are through with games, right? Don't believe it. You may be playing in the big game most of us play in—the *Treading Water Game.* The rules are easy. You earn money. This qualifies you for government assistance in the form of taxes and inflation. If more income is earned, your taxes tend to go up. Whether you earn more or not, during periods of inflation, your purchasing power goes down. In other words, how long can you tread water? Sure, the government now adjusts your income taxes to inflation. But what the government giveth, it usually taketh away somewhere else. Since there is no evidence that the government will operate on less money than before, you're still treading water. And you can bet your snorkel that Uncle Sam is offsetting any tax breaks by raising taxes somewhere else. Consider the water deep until such time that you can touch the bottom. In the meantime, you can't afford to manage family finances fairly well in this game. Those dollars must be managed *very* well. A budget can help get the most out of them.

But the greatest benefit of budgeting is obtaining the things you want, which just happens to fit nicely with the best reason for managing money in the first place. If you receive a lot of sympathy along the way, why not? While everyone thinks you are sacrificing to stick to a budget, you can work on a wish list: the new car, the vacation to the place you've always wanted to visit, the new clothes to wear in style, or evenings out on the town—all of these are wants. So are the special times with family or friends, the pleasure of helping others, or simply doing the things you like to do.

Owning your own business, taking tennis lessons, or going back to college may be just what you have always wanted to do. And why not? Goals are limited only by imagination. A family goal can be a cabin at a favorite place to get away on carefree weekends. If so, put a cabin on your list. Or, you might long for something as simple as more free time. Money can buy time when someone is hired to do all the little jobs that seem to claim your freedom. If more free time is a goal, put it on the list. Even a dream home—one with a big backyard and a swimming pool—can be on a family's wish list.

Wants come in all sizes, shapes, and colors. Financial security, good health, or adding a room on the house might be among your family's choices. We don't all want the same things in life. The items on your

INFLATION
TAXES

family's list won't be the same as another family's wants. This should provide some idea of how ridiculous it is to try to keep up with the neighbors. You will do better pursuing your own choices, as exotic or crazy as they may be.

My neighbor is looking for several rolls of barbed wire, the kind they used in World War II. This, he figures, will keep kids, dogs, extraterrestrials, and any other trespassers off his property, allowing his shrubbery and trees a better-than-even chance of survival. Needless to say, coils of barbed wire are high on his wish list, although I, for one, couldn't care less about barbed wire. Your choices are not necessarily the same as mine, your neighbor's, or even what Aunt Harriet thinks you should have in life.

I never realized just how unique our own preferences in life really are, until a friend of mine who works as a mechanic helped me to understand. He enjoys restoring old cars in his spare time. While I was watching him tinker with one of his cars one day, I asked him:

"George, why don't you buy a new car instead of fixing up these old clunkers? You certainly can afford one."

"Sure, I could afford one," he said, pausing and looking up at me as if this was some kind of answer.

"Do you see that nut over there?" he said, pointing to his neighbor, who was busily washing his new automobile.

"What's so nutty about him?" I asked.

"Well, every year he buys a new car. This old car of mine will take me anywhere his new one will go and some places it won't. Why should I buy a new car?"

My friend George wouldn't own a new car if it was given to him. He enjoys the challenge of repairing an old engine so that it runs like a new one. And he is proud of his vintage vehicles. On the other hand, his neighbor has no intention of owning an automobile where there is the slightest chance he will need a wrench. He thinks George is the nut. Although both men desire the same thing—a car—they have completely different goals. Yet each one is getting what he wants. Isn't this the least any of us should do for ourselves?

True, you won't get everything right away. But the waiting period can be shortened with a budget to remind you of family choices and to keep you moving steadily on track toward them. Since life is full of surprises, there are plenty of distractions ahead. If you get off course—and you will—a budget can offer warnings that you are sidetracked. It can also show how to get back on course. This is one advantage that should not be taken lightly. Knowing family goals and making a plan to get them can put you in a position that is light years ahead of where you would be if you were spending money aimlessly and waiting for family wants to appear on the horizon.

2

Your Dark Past

Here you are, ready to start identifying goals, analyzing priorities, and exploring innovative ways to get your wish list, when what should turn up but your dark past. Needless to say, you aren't too excited about digging up the financial past; particularly if you've been playing the *Boomerang* or *Rebound* games. Unfortunately, you must know where you have been to know where you are going. This means figuring out how the money was spent and received last year. If you feel this could be a traumatic disclosure, peace treaties can be signed in advance guaranteeing each family member's safety. A simple form like this one should do:

I, ____ solemnly swear (affirm) that I will not get angry when I learn how ____ threw away our money last year.

      SIGNED ____

With this assurance, everyone can face the family's money past, come what may.

How The Money Was Spent

Begin with your checkbook register. This is the record in front of a checkbook that keeps track of checks written and balances remaining.

13

THE BANK

It's also your ticket to the monthly game of wits between you and your bank statement, commonly known as "reconciling" the checkbook. The mysteries of past finances can be discovered in this little record. To unlock these secrets, employ the tools any first-rate detective would use. These include, among other things, a probing mind and a calculator. With an investigative attitude and enough checkbook registers to cover the last twelve months, you can make a summary of past spending that will unlock the mysteries. Simply set up categories such as food, household, transportation, and other classes of spending to record where the money went. Then list the amount of each check in the category to which it belongs. Many families have more than one checking account. If your family is one of them, list all checks from every account. If you can't find those old checkbook registers, use the cancelled checks returned in past bank statements to make a summary.

Anyone who has ever tried to fit his spending into the average American family's categories already knows his family isn't average. These "average" categories are for families with two and one-half children and simple last names like Doe. Invariably, when you try to fit your spending into these or anyone else's categories, they don't fit. In Wyoming, for example, people don't spend much money for the subway. And residents of New York City don't buy a lot of horse feed. This is reason enough to create your own categories. As a practical matter, you don't need one category for shoelaces and another for soap. Throw these and a couple of other million items into a household category. You need a reasonable breakdown of spending, not a complete audit. Beyond this caution, feel free to make up categories to fit your family's crazy spending.

The idea, of course, is to list all checks in the correct category and then add up the numbers to see how the money was spent. This is usually easier said than done. Some stores sell everything from cat food to car parts and you may not remember what was purchased eleven months ago, let alone last week. Worse, there may be someone in the family with a talent for spending money and leaving no trace of evidence for where it went. But you are not wearing your Sherlock Holmes hat for nothing. To handle this mysterious spending, do what any self-respecting sleuth would do: stall. Buy a little time to think by setting up an "Unknown" category. Here you can put checks written out to "Cash," checks to stores that sell everything from soup to nuts, and any other spending that can't be traced for the moment. Later on, after you have listed the bulk of last year's payments—the easier checks to list—you can come back and solve the "Unknowns." This gives your probing mind time to warm up.

You will love those old checks written to pay former gas or electric bills. Why? Because these checks pay for only one thing—gas or electricity, as the case may be. This makes it easy to find the correct category for them. It is the checks that paid for different things at the same time that you will regard with the affection reserved for cockroaches. Fortune being what it is, these different things bought and paid for with one check seldom belong in the same category. To get them in the right place, the amount paid must be separated according to each type of purchase made. For instance, the checks that paid credit card statements may have involved several different stores and types of spending. Dig out old card statements and review them to see what your money actually bought. It may not be easy; especially if you made payments on charge accounts and did not pay the full amount due each month. Still, with a little investigative work, those payments can be broken down to fit them into the correct categories.

You are not in ground school to get your wings in bookkeeping. Don't worry about finding every last cent. The idea is to solve the mystery of your past finances. When finished, you will want to see a general picture of where the money went. This is detective work. Go back and review those "Unknowns". If you can't remember where checks made out to "Cash" went, try thinking about what your family usually does with cash. If you can't break down the checks written to pay on a charge account, find out how much was paid to the card company for all of last year. Then look through your old statements to make an estimate of the amount spent for the year on clothes, entertainment, and other classes of spending. If half of your expenditure was for clothing, assign half of the yearly total paid to the clothes category. And do the same for other classes of spending represented in card statements.

At our house, it was not the money we spent on clothes or entertainment that was last year's deep, dark secret. It was the money spent at our favorite store where the clerks knock themselves out thinking up such colorful words as "merchandise" or "items" to describe charges made on our credit card. We solved this mysterious spending by thinking about what we usually buy at this store and looking at the time in the month or year our purchase was made. As it turned out, those "items" bought in the middle of the month were usually related to personal care, like shaving cream or shampoo. Purchases near holidays were often gifts. And one late day in August, my wife undoubtedly cleaned out the store purchasing school supplies for the kids, not to mention the cleaning job she did on our bank account.

Checks to relatives, people who you don't remember, and stores that you never heard of may be part of your dark past. Solving these mysteries means looking for clues. Any detective skills short of cross-examining family members under a bright, hot light are fair game.

When the "Unknowns" have been solved and all payments listed, add up the amounts in each category for a grand total of your family's spending. This is how you blew your money last year. Congratulations!

How Money Was Received Last Year

Discovering how money was received is less painful than learning how it was spent. It's also easier, unless money is coming in from every direction. Use your checkbook register again to list past deposits on your summary. Paycheck deposits should be easy to recognize. Deposits from such activities as wheeling and dealing, horse trading, and other vices are more difficult to find. Still, with remedial detective skills, you should be able to list them all.

The Big Picture

Now, you can step back and look at the forest instead of the trees. Daily decisions on money matters are the trees. The forest is what they all add up to. Depending on how your money was used, this view will either be appealing or it won't be. From this vantage point, you have the perspective to make needed changes. Besides, why go to all this trouble of digging up your financial past? Not for the excitement. Take time to review how your money was spent and received last year. Here is where uncovering the mysteries of past finances can pay off.

What spending amounts surprised you? Some people are absolutely flabbergasted at the amounts spent in some categories. This is the kind of surprise that comes from learning that your family spent seven thousand dollars on food last year. It's the most amazing thing. You can buy the $1.20-a-pound ground beef all year long and never know you are paying seven thousand dollars a year on food or that this amount represents say, one-fifth of your annual income. The important thing is not that this amount was spent or even that it might come to twenty percent of all the money available last year. What matters is knowing the amount so that you can decide to keep spending this way or make a change in spending habits. You may prefer paying less for food and having the flexibility to spend more on other things. Or, you might be deliriously happy about the amount paid for food last year (though I can't imagine why). Either way, look closely at those yearly amounts in each category. It is not every day that you see the cumulative effects of past money decisions. When you do, a larger perspective of family money matters is gained than if you continue buying the $1.20-a-pound ground beef week in and week out. Old spending habits can't be changed without first recognizing them and knowing their effect on your finances.

How much of your money last year went toward payments on debts? If heavily in debt, you probably paid a large portion of your money to creditors, leaving few dollars for other things. Comparing debt payments with other spending shows who has the most influence in your family finances: you or your creditors. If it turns out that creditors have all the sway, you should change this situation or invite them for lunch. If they are controlling the money, they might as well eat at your house too. In the meantime, knowing the amount spent on debt payments last year can do wonders for your resolve to make a needed change.

How much "choice" spending did your family have last year? Anyone who has bought something over his spouse's objections knows about choices. He can also tell you much about the consequences. But the trick is to decide which categories were choice spending and which ones were fixed, meaning the money had to be paid or else. If two mobsters carrying violin cases were waiting outside in the event you failed to pay the money, call it fixed spending. Buying a dining room set because a salesman made an offer you couldn't refuse was obviously a matter of choice. Seldom, however, will the decision be this clear-cut. Take mortgage payments, for example. Are they fixed or choice spending? The answer depends on how a family feels about their home. One family might consider a mortgage payment as choice spending, because they feel renting is always an option. In short, they choose to own rather than rent. Conversely, another family might find renting loathsome, in which case they may think of the monthly mortgage payment as fixed spending. Label each category as fixed or choice spending, according to your feeling about each type. By comparing these divisions, you will learn how much flexibility existed in past money matters. This will also reveal attitudes toward different types of spending. Sometimes it is old attitudes about spending that keep us from making needed changes.

Did your family save any money last year? If you are scurrying for an answer to this question, you probably overlooked your savings. But don't feel badly. Most of us think of savings as something altogether different from spending, or at least the kind of spending we do on shopping excursions. But your savings account is money spent on your family's future. And you, super sleuth, need to find the amount saved last year. It may have been deposited directly to your bank account through a payroll savings plan or some other enforced method. If it turns out that a microscope is needed to see this amount, consider changing your savings habits. You have tipped the scales in favor of the present at the expense of your family's future. If the amount adds up to zero, you paid everyone else but yourself.

What spending would you like to change? This is not the place to decide who should be shot at sunrise. This is where a family decides if they like the way their money was used last year and if not, what changes should be made. Rarely will everyone in the family be pleased about the way money was spent last year. But for every type of spending earmarked for change, consider the alternative. You may not be thrilled about installment payments on the car, but are you prepared to walk? Soul-searching questions like this one insure that wise changes are made later.

Where did your money come from last year? A family's summary should include all money sources. These sources are usually divided into groups, such as dividends, interest, capital gains, wages, and other types of income, depending on who wants to know. But the government isn't doing the asking here. You are asking. And this kind of detailed information is seldom necessary. In our family, we divide our sources of money inflow into two groups: routine money sources and interesting sources. Looking back at last year, the sources that regularly added money to your account, such as a paycheck, are usually expected and not particularly interesting, although if you routinely received money from sources like oil well royalties, the rest of us would find that interesting. But often as not, the little ways that money was received are the interesting ones, such as proceeds from a garage sale last year, or a deposit made from those nifty shares of blue–chip stock that were sold, or even the extra money earned while moonlighting on weekends. These sources are intriguing because they provide ideas for earning extra income next year. They are also interesting because even though they may come in small figures, those dollars can add up to sizable amounts. The next time your family is brainstorming for ways to earn additional money, these interesting money sources in your past are the first ones that should be remembered.

Routine money sources are usually important, though infinitely boring. Fifty-two weekly deposits of a paycheck deserve a yawn at best. But these income sources become interesting immediately after they vanish. Which is why you should consider them wonderfully routine, like postcards from your mother-in-law that are mailed from foreign countries. Looking at the ways money was received last year provides a panoramic view of family income. This shows how the family's money sources came together to supply the money received. This view is revealing and useful for future planning.

After digging up your financial past, both you and your family are now acquainted—perhaps for the first time—with how the money was received and spent last year. This could reveal many family secrets that may keep you at each other's throats into the next century. Drag out your peace treaties. You have been looking at the past. Budgeting looks at the future. To change directions, you will need to become a calm, rational, and cooperative family. Never mind what the neighbors will think. If only for the moment, reason must prevail.

Table 1

TIPS FOR MAKING A SUMMARY OF PAST FINANCES

Digging up a family's money past is not a task reserved strictly for Mom and Dad. Kids can sort old checks, add numbers, and discover things that you never dreamed would show up. They can also learn how much money is being spent on them, which should be enlightening for everyone. Make this task of digging up the past a family affair and you can make it a fun project. Besides, children make good detectives. You never know when one of them will use the new math to discover a refund due. Stranger things have happened.

Here are some additional tips to make the task of drafting a summary easier. Use them in good health, keeping your peace treaties nearby.

Work backwards through the last twelve months to list spending. This method deals with last month's payments first, which should be the easiest to remember. Later on, as your sleuthing skills improve, you'll be able to find where the money went in earlier months.

If you absolutely cannot solve an "Unknown" in past spending, make a guess. It probably won't make that much difference in the general picture of your past finances. The sizable amounts are the ones likely to be remembered because they make an impression on both your memory and bank account.

Keep separate monthly totals of both past spending and income. This helps identify payment and income cycles in your money past. This information is helpful later when you are trying to predict future spending and income cycles.

Some of last year's money transactions may not have flowed through your bank account and as a result, are not recorded in checkbook registers. Say, for instance, you took out a loan and didn't deposit the proceeds in a checking account, but instead used the money to pay cash for some new purchase. In this case, the loan and spending won't be on the summary unless you remember to include them. Try to recall money transactions that are a part of last year's financial activity but that may not be represented in old checkbook registers.

For a shortcut to listing the money paid out last year, separate old checks in past bank statements into separate piles—one for each type of spending represented. Then add up the total of each pile of checks. This avoids a lot of the paperwork by allowing you to write only the monthly totals on a summary instead of listing each check. This shortcut works well for those checks that fit only into one category. List individually those checks that must be broken into different spending types.

Don't wait around until New Year's Eve to make a summary. You can start a budget any time during the year by going back twelve months in your money past. By waiting for the end of the year, you will be wasting time. Besides, January may not be the best month to turn over a new leaf in your finances. You may have already promised more than you can deliver with other New Year's resolutions.

Table 2

HOW YOU BLEW YOUR MONEY LAST YEAR

SPENDING CATEGORIES	JAN	FEB	MAR	APR	MAY	JUN	JUL	AUG	SEP	OCT	NOV	DEC	YEAR
TOTAL SPENDING													

HOW YOU GOT THE MONEY FOR ALL THIS EXTRAVAGANT SPENDING

INCOMING DOLLARS	JAN	FEB	MAR	APR	MAY	JUN	JUL	AUG	SEP	OCT	NOV	DEC	YEAR
TOTAL INCOMING MONEY													

3

A Family Wish List

If all your income goes to support Spot in the manner to which he is accustomed, you probably won't have much left for investing in his future, not to mention your own. Of course, Spot won't be worried about his future until he reaches it. And he will fight to the last dog biscuit to keep living the good life now. This leaves a couple of choices: warn Spot not to bite the hand that feeds him, or buy more dog food.

Or you can do as I do and let the family council decide. Choosing wants is a project for the whole family, and everyone should have some say in it. The family council is where the family democratically decides on a list of goals for the coming year. It is also where members vote on what comes first and last on the list and at the same time, chop off any notions Spot may have about eating steak every night while the rest of the family dines on leftovers.

Ideally this family negotiating session is where diplomacy prevails and trade-offs and deals are made. But as it usually turns out, everyone has his own idea of what the family's preferences should be. Kids think nothing of putting their favorite desires in front of life's little necessities, like keeping the house. Which is why I say: decide on necessities first, then deal with everyone's ideas. Even so, you'd better develop some bargaining skills. Any four-year-old knows he needs allies to get a new tricycle at the top of the family's list. And older family members are usually not far behind in making this discovery.

This often leads to friendships within the family that would not be possible under normal circumstances. And since any new-found camaraderie among former foes can be a threat to your new golf clubs, be prepared to bargain in your own interests.

Don't invoke the "I know best" rule. You don't know best, at least not without the rest of the family's vote. And Spot may seek his revenge with a few well-placed teeth marks unless he receives a fair hearing at the family council. Worse, goals that don't have the support of the family majority are doomed.

Now, sit down and list your family's goals on a sheet of paper. In an hour or two—presto!—you will have maybe, three goals. And two of them will be similar, if not the same thing. Next, try making a list of the things you want, using no more than two or three mail order catalogs to get started. Soon you will need more paper. All of which proves it is easier to think of goals as wants.

To simplify matters even more, think of them as *future* wants. Since you must deal with the immediate and distant future, these time frames can be addressed as short-term and long-term wants. You may wish to buy a new car this year. This is a short-term want. You may also prefer living your retirement years in comfort rather than sifting through old garbage cans looking for a meal, which is a long-term want.

Short-term wants are seldom vague. For instance, there is nothing vague about the new train set for which your son would do anything to acquire. Ask him. He will tell you all about this train and may even promise to wash the dishes for the next twelve years to get it. Anyone who makes such promises knows what he wants. If you doubt this, buy the wrong train set, the little one with the engine that doesn't smoke and the caboose that doesn't look the way a first-grader thinks a caboose ought to look. You will quickly discover that your son's desire is crystal clear in his mind. In the same way, there is nothing vague about the ski vacation your family would love to take in Aspen next year or the new drapes and carpet for the living room.

But when it comes to long-term wants, the fog sets in. What is comfort in your retirement years? Winning the state lottery, maybe. Or it could be finding long-lost, rich relatives wherever they may be. But comfort means different things to different people. Unless your idea of comfort is a bench in the city park, you'd better start being more specific. Comfort could mean a retirement villa on the beach. Or it might be a paid-up mortgage on the house and a retirement income that will allow you to travel. Whatever comfort means to you, make it specific. Instead of "we want to be wealthy," your goal might be two hundred thousand dollars to retire on in twenty years. This provides a concrete target. In turn, a target forces you to think about how your goal of comfort will be achieved. Whether you save for it, invest for it, or sell hubcaps for it, make sure the method requires action on your part. Don't wait for the money to fall out of an armored truck.

And how are you going to save enough to buy a retirement villa on the beach? It's often enough trouble trying to make ends meet from one paycheck to the next, let alone saving money. But millions of families manage to get by on less and save some money for their future. With this knowledge and a commitment to put away a small amount of savings each month, you can do the impossible, too. And with this advice, you are back to following armored trucks.

Worse, you are also wasting a precious asset—time. If you consistently save money a little at the time, those small amounts of money will grow with the compounding effect of interest. By putting them into an account where they are not taxed, such as an individual retirement account (IRA), you won't be sharing them with Uncle Sam. Admittedly, IRAs may not be around much longer, but if you still qualify for one, it's a great place for retirement savings. Through an IRA, the government provides an incentive to save dollars to obtain a retirement villa or any other retirement goals. This is a double incentive that adds up to a big bonanza, if people take advantage of the opportunity. Not only does savings earn tax-free interest this way, but you also receive a deduction on income taxes for the amount put in your account each year. True, you will pay taxes on the money when it is taken out. But by then you should be in a lower tax bracket, living comfortably in your retirement villa. Starting at age thirty-five and saving twenty-five dollars a week in an IRA, you would have $247,361 at the age of sixty-five, assuming that ten percent interest is earned on savings. Without an IRA and the tax advantages that go with it, you would end up with $132,872 at age sixty-five, figuring the same interest rate and a thirty percent tax bracket. Which of these two amounts would you rather have?

And right away, people get the wrong idea about saving money. They figure they can put their money into an IRA or some other form of savings, and sit back to watch their money start piling up. But compounding doesn't work that way. Instead, it plods along, building up your stockpile slowly at first. Inside your savings is a little manager that checks his calendar and tells his workers every so often to add money to your account.

"Add forty-two cents to the account, Harry."

Next month he'll tell Harry to add maybe, eighty-three cents. Meanwhile, you and Harry are going crazy with these piddling amounts. But later on, when Harry is old and you are getting older too, the manager will tell Harry to add three thousand to the account. Then Harry will have dollar signs in his eyes and you will be impressed. In the meantime, by saving, you steadily gain on retirement goals each day. Money earns money. Later on, when those dollars start piling up, you *can* be amazed. Meanwhile, by getting started, what appears to be out of reach today may be within your grasp tomorrow.

Of course, by the time you reach retirement age, there is a good chance that a villa on the beach will cost several times the amount it costs now, considering inflation. Or, a retirement income that looks adequate today may not mean very much when you retire. In this case, don't be concerned with saving one amount when you may need more to buy your wants. Simply adjust your sights a little higher. And take a bow for discovering that the risk is not setting your goals too high. It is setting them too low.

The last thing needed in the distant future is to discover that, with inflation, your savings won't buy the back porch, let alone a retirement villa. In this case, savings chase after price increases on your retirement goals, while you stand by and lose the race. This spectator sport is about as exciting as watching snow melt. As long as you are betting on the outcome, you should know a few tricks to hedge the bet and win this race.

My six-year-old son, Tony, taught me one of these tricks while he was learning the savings game. His problem was that he did not receive enough allowance to buy his long-desired goal, a new bike. Not one to give up easily, he saved his weekly allowance diligently, foregoing the luxuries of ice cream cones and other goodies longer than anyone thought possible. My wife and I were in a quandary, watching this little kid save a small amount at a time for a bike that would take untold weeks to accumulate enough to buy. We worried for naught. He marched in one day, announced his latest purchase—a new bike—and asked us to come see it. It seems he acquired sufficient funds to entice his older sister to part with her bike in trade for his cash: a bargain if I ever saw one. We threw in a can of spray paint to consummate the deal and settled back to take a brighter look at our own monthly savings going toward long-term goals. In the meantime, we have learned to keep a sharper eye out for early bargains on these goals.

If this idea seems far-fetched, you ought to meet a businessman I know. He believes that people don't have to live their life according to the government's timeclock. You can retire when you choose to do it. In the meantime, he advises finding bargains on retirement wants and buying them early. A few years ago, he bought a condominium in a well-known community where retired folks congregate. He wasn't planning to retire for several more years, so I asked him:

"Why did you buy a condo now?"

"Why not?" he replied. "Just because I don't want to retire now doesn't mean that I won't retire someday. When I do, my wife and I expect to live there and soak up the sunshine."

"Well, that makes sense," I said, curious about the idea. "How did you do it?"

"Easy," he said. "We took out a subscription to the community's newspaper and watched the local real estate listings for a while. When we saw an opportunity to buy a condo at a bargain, we took it."

"But how did you afford it?" I persisted.

"Well, we used some of our savings for the down payment and we hired a management firm to rent out our condo during the year. Except for the two weeks each year when we spend our family vacation there, they keep the place rented to cover the monthly mortgage payments."

What a brilliant idea, I thought. Here is a couple who is purchasing their long-term goals early by using other people's money to help pay for them. Not only did someone else—a lender—put up the mortgage money, but the renters are making the payments. This couple ended up with a retirement condo using very few of their own dollars. Moreover, they have already been offered a better price than they paid for their condominium to sell it. Are they selling? Absolutely not. Why sell when they already have one of their retirement goals?

True, some money reserves are helpful to take advantage of these kind of opportunities. But you don't always need savings to get in on deals like this one. Even so, with some reserves of your own, you will have more opportunities from which to choose. This makes building up money reserves a worthwhile project. And the building process can be speeded up by investing. Its one way to win the race with inflation to reach lofty goals.

This is a race very much like the hare and tortoise. Like the hare, inflation tends to run fast for awhile and then slow down. When inflation is running slowly is a time when you need savings or investments to keep trudging along as any good tortoise should do. Races are won this way. They are also won by having more than one entry at the track. Since your family is betting on the outcome, why not have both savings and investments in the race, improving the odds of winning? Many investments can trudge along faster than savings. And some of them can trudge along so fast that they stay ahead of inflation. Investment opportunities abound these days. The difficult task is picking the right investment from the tantalizing choices available: mutual funds, stocks, options, commodity futures, bonds, government securities, money markets, investment trusts, real estate, rare coins, precious metals, oil and gas drilling partnerships, equipment leases, annuities—you name it and you can probably invest in it. The important thing to remember here is that reaching long-term goals often requires investing for them.

Things You Never Knew Were Wants

You have numerous goals for the coming year that don't require binoculars to see. An adequate food budget is one. If you prefer the finer culinary tastes—steak versus beans—include this preference on your list. Even the little things often taken for granted are wants. There is nothing like having the heat turned off in the winter to make you appreciate the comforts of a warm and cozy home. If you'd rather not test this for yourself, include warm and cozy as a short-term goal. And don't forget those things already owned; to retain them will require some funds. These may include keeping up the payments on a home, a car, or the silverware. They're still wants. So are the special events that are overlooked at budget time, like Christmas toys and gifts. When the season rolls around, you will remember these wants. The trick is to remember them in advance.

Balancing The Time Frames

Since few of us can have all our wishes granted immediately, we are forced to make choices. And invariably, the decision comes down to choosing between short-term and long-term goals. To understand how this works, picture yourself as a contestant on a television show. Behind the red curtain are your immediate wants, including the five days and four nights in Rio. Behind the blue curtain are distant and boring desires, like retirement income. And the green curtain is where you take a chance. Now decide. As the seconds tick off reasons for not choosing long-term goals will come to mind. The reason most often picked is the theory that you probably won't live long enough to collect on them. Don't bet on it. Millions of people reach retirement each year, and the odds are good that you will, too. When you arrive at the golden years, you will either be glad that you provided for your future or wish the government would raise Social Security benefits. On the other hand, you can live like a monk today and pursue long-term goals exclusively. In this case, you sacrifice the wild nights in Rio. Or, you can obtain the best of both time frames by striking a happy balance between the long and the short of it. Whereupon, you should pick the green curtain—the one with a year's supply of lawn fertilizer in front of it. Behind this curtain is that happy balance and your choice of both immediate and distant goals.

Pricing A Wish List

Wants are the family's shopping list for the future. At the checkout counter, you will need to pay for them. If you can't pay, they are placed back on the shelf. One way to avoid this embarrassing scene is to know the price of family wants in advance. This can be accomplished by looking at what some of them cost last year. Your warm and cozy goal should have a price equal to last year's heating bill, plus maybe, some adjustment. Keeping the house means paying the rent or mortgage for another year. These kind of wants are easy to price. Others require more imagination and arithmetic. A retirement nest egg, for example, has a price equal to the amount of savings or investment needed each year to reach it. Depending on how many years you have remaining until retirement, figure out the amount that must be invested or saved each year to accumulate your nest egg. If you plan to purchase a new car in the coming year, estimate its price based on what you expect to pay in cash. If you plan to finance it, add the monthly installments to the down payment for next year's price. The piano lessons for your daughter should cost the weekly price of the lessons times the number of weeks you expect to endure the practice sessions. Then throw in a few dollars for earplugs. Just as your family's wants are unique and not exactly like any other family's, so is the price paid for them. This rules out the possibility of borrowing some handy guidebook from your neighbor to price them.

Make sure family wants are priced in terms of how much they will cost for the complete year ahead. This makes it easier to draft a plan to obtain them. For those items on your list that will require financing, include their total price as well. This helps identify those choices that will affect future budgets to pay for them. And don't worry about whether or not you can afford the price. You are not at the checkout counter yet—you are still browsing. For the moment, it is only important to know the price. Paying it will be dealt with in your plan.

Naturally, the idea is to buy the important things first. Then later, when shopping again, pick up the minor ones. This means your family must set some guidelines to decide the importance of each choice on the list. To make this job easier, separate necessities first. Nominations for these might include warm and cozy, lights at night, water on tap, and others. Once these are out of the way, decide the priority of the rest of your wants by numbering them in their order of importance to the family. If you need more help, divide choices into groups; then deal with one group at a time. How you divide them doesn't matter, but by dealing with one group at a time, it is often easier to decide what comes first and last on the list.

What should your priorities be? That is up to you. Each family has their own preference in choosing one want over another. Just remember to consider the effects of choices when you make them. It's one thing to have your new golf clubs voted to the bottom of the list, but finding your future in this position is not worthwhile.

Not surprisingly, Spot has his own ideas about what the family's priorities should be. This is no guarantee, however, that he will have anything to do with your first family council. If you have been making all the money decisions in the past, Spot and everyone else may view this session with considerable skepticism. And for good reason. You

made all the money decisions in the past. Why should things be any different now? The first task is to win over the skeptics.

Here's how we did it. A few days before our first family council, my wife and I posted a list of wants on the refrigerator door, filling in our own favorite choices. The kids thought the whole affair was a trick to lower their allowances. We told them to fill in their own wants under their names anyway. The first day, no one signed up. Day two saw an occasional huddle around the refrigerator, but still no one signed up. The third day, the kids waited till evening to ask if this was some kind of hoax. We explained that it was not and told them how the council worked. For good measure, we threw in the "what-have-you-got-to-lose" theory. The next day our family's list was overflowing. Even the neighbors were waiting to see the outcome.

You may not face this kind of skepticism. But you had better make certain that everyone's choices are on the negotiating table. The suggestions that follow will help prepare a well-rounded agenda. Add to these your own ideas or pick and choose from the list to select those wants that fit your family's lifestyle. With a specially tailored list, your family stands not only to gain their favorite choices, but also to learn a great deal about the family finances.

Table 3

SUGGESTIONS FOR SHORT-TERM WANTS

Necessities	Warm and cozy, water on tap, lights at night, an adequate food supply, among others.
Allowances	Having some money to spend as you please.
Avoiding Jail	Paying income taxes.
Camp	Getting rid of the kids next summer.
Clothes	For style, comfort, or fashion to fit the occasion.
Disaster Insurance	Life, health, property, and liability to avoid or soften the calamities that may come your way.
Education	Expanding the family's horizons.
Emergency Cash Fund	Three months worth of income saved up in case the boss goes bananas and you need to look for another job.
Entertainment	Enjoying the things you like to do.
Getting Out Of Hock	Paying off old debts, including credit card balances.
Good Health	Paying the doctor, dentist, or others to keep you going.
Hobbies	Paying for fishing, hunting, stamp collecting, and other activities that are supposed to pay for themselves.
Investments	Putting money aside to earn more money in the short run.
Keeping Your Property	Paying assessments and taxes to avoid bidding on your own goods at the courthouse steps.
More Choice Spending	(*See* "Getting Out Of Hock")
Special Events	Christmas gifts, the class reunion, or the trip home.
Special Projects	The addition on the house, do–it–yourself projects, or building a better mousetrap.
Transportation	Getting from "A" to "B" in style, comfort, and in one piece.
Worthy Causes	Giving to your church or favorite charity, or helping others.

Table 4

SUGGESTIONS FOR LONG–TERM WANTS

College For The Kids	Do you intend to pay the whole cost or let them earn a portion of it? *See* Table 8.
Dream Home	Saving for a down payment or the additional equity needed to move up.
Investments	Setting money aside for investments where you can come back later and find you have a bundle.
Retirement	Saving an amount for retirement not provided by investments, social security benefits, pension plans, or other income sources. *See* Table 12.
Vacation Retreat	A summer cabin at the lake, a condo at the ski slopes, or a motor home to take you where you'd like to go.

Table 5

SUGGESTIONS FOR THE FAMILY COUNCIL

Always separate necessities first. You can count on some family members to determine that the smaller the number of necessities, the better their chances of getting their own favorite items. Don't trade off a necessity your family can't do without.

Always make certain everyone in the family has at least some of their favorite choices near the top of the list. If your family council doesn't work to everyone's benefit, it's not working properly.

Look at all the ways you spent money last year. Did you buy your wants? By looking at last year's spending, you may discover some forgotten items that you may not wish to forget this year.

When your family has selected a list of wants for the coming year and put them on a priority scale, check to see if the list is balanced. This means looking at the list in total, not just each item. If implementing the list will require a big change in your family's lifestyle, make certain everyone is prepared for it. It's easy to focus attention on individual choices and overlook the big picture of what your list will mean.

Are you having trouble seeing what long-term goals will be? Read the magazines the retired crowd reads, such as *Modern Maturity, Fifty-Plus, Dynamic Years,* and others. It's a likely conclusion that some of your interests will be similar to the things they are doing.

Table 6

THE FAMILY WANTS

Family Choices	Total Price	This Yrs Price	Importance Rating
Necessities:			
________	________	________	
________	________	________	
________	________	________	
________	________	________	
________	________	________	
________	________	________	
________	________	________	
Short-term wants:			
________	________	________	________
________	________	________	________
________	________	________	________
________	________	________	________
________	________	________	________
________	________	________	________
________	________	________	________
________	________	________	________
________	________	________	________
________	________	________	________
________	________	________	________
________	________	________	________
________	________	________	________
________	________	________	________
________	________	________	________
________	________	________	________
________	________	________	________
Long-term wants:			
________	________	________	________
________	________	________	________
________	________	________	________
________	________	________	________
________	________	________	________
________	________	________	________
________	________	________	________
________	________	________	________
Total	________	________	

Table 7

HOW TO MAKE YOUR SAVINGS GROW

1. Shop interest rates to obtain the best rate of interest on your money.

2. Pay attention to compounding—the frequency at which banks, savings and loans, credit unions, or others pay interest on interest. Compounded annually, quarterly, monthly, daily or continuously—in this order it goes from lousy to great as far as savings are concerned.

3. Make regular contributions to savings like clockwork, rain or shine. When you are about to convince yourself that a payment to your savings can be skipped, think of all the reasons why you should pay everyone else first. If any of these reasons are worth putting your family last, think again!

4. Use your savings to remind a banker that you deserve the good person, V.I.P., or dog days discount—or any other breaks on interest rates when borrowing. Less money going out to pay interest means more money available for savings.

5. Don't save money without a purpose in mind. It's tough to be committed to saving money without a goal. It is even more difficult to convince the rest of the family to save when you have no clear reason for doing it.

6. Get to know a banker and make him a friend. If anyone knows the money game, he does. Ask for his advice and counsel to find the best type of savings investment.

7. Think of some other smart idea to make your savings grow and write it here. Then you will have seven good ideas for saving along with the good luck that ought to go with it.

Table 8

THE HIGH COST OF COLLEGE AND PAYING FOR IT
(In Case Junior Doesn't Become Rich & Famous At An Early Age)

Age Of Child Now	Four Yr Cost — Public	Monthly Savings Required To Pay Total Cost	Monthly Savings Required To Pay 75% Of The Cost
1	$44,353	$116.92	$ 87.69
2	$42,241	$120.96	$ 90.72
3	$40,230	$125.51	$ 94.13
4	$38,314	$130.66	$ 97.99
5	$36,489	$136.52	$102.39
6	$34,752	$143.25	$107.44
7	$33,097	$151.05	$113.29
8	$31,521	$160.20	$120.15
9	$30,020	$171.05	$128.29
10	$28,590	$184.12	$138.09
11	$27,229	$200.15	$150.11
12	$25,932	$220.25	$165.19
13	$24,697	$246.17	$184.63
14	$23,521	$280.80	$210.60
15	$22,401	$329.40	$247.05
16	$21,335	$402.43	$301.82
17	$20,319	$524.31	$393.23
18	$19,351	$768.33	$576.25

Based on 1982–83 mean college cost of $4388 per year — public college adjusted for inflation at 5% annually. Costs include tuition, books and supplies, room and board, personal expenses, and transportation. Cost amounts rounded. Savings based on 5% after-tax interest earned, compounded monthly. The table assumes that savings will continue for two years after the child enters college. Actual costs and savings required may vary, depending on inflation and interest rates.

Table 9

SEVEN NOT-SO-EASY STEPS TO FIGURE RETIREMENT NEEDS

1. Decide the age at which you will retire and find the number of years remaining before reaching this age.

2. Make a budget for your first year of retirement using last year's spending as a guide. Adjust each spending category to project expenses during retirement. Include any spending not reflected in last year's categories that may occur during retirement. Don't worry about adjusting for inflation yet.

3. Now you can worry. Adjust the total of your retirement budget for likely inflation during the years remaining until you retire. An accountant can help you do this or use the inflation-factors provided on page 42. Here's an example using a factor from the table: A $30,000 estimated retirement budget adjusted for twenty years of 4% inflation would equate to a $65,700 budget at retirement. (Using the inflation-factors provided, find the factor 2.19 under a four percent inflation rate and across from twenty years. Multiply 2.19 times $30,000.)

4. Find the annual income amounts you can expect from social security benefits, company pension plans, and other retirement income sources, not including savings or investments. A social security office can assist you in making this estimate. Check with an employer, union, or association for needed figures from a pension plan.

5. Determine how much additional yearly income will be needed from savings or investments to maintain your estimated retirement budget. Subtract the total income derived in step four from the total of your retirement budget. The difference is the annual income that must be provided from savings or investments to cover retirement living expenses.

6. Determine the amount of savings or investments that must be accumulated to provide this additional income during retirement. Simply divide the total income from step five by the return on savings or investments that you expect to earn. For instance, if forty thousand dollars of yearly income is needed in step five, and your savings will earn a ten percent return, divide $40,000 by 10% for the total savings needed ($400,000).

7. Find the amount in the table on page 42 that you must save or invest each week or month until retirement to accumulate the savings needed. Then save or invest this amount.

Table 10

SAMPLE WORKSHEET FOR RETIREMENT PLANNING

Step 1
Age you will retire _________________
Years remaining until you reach this age _________________

Step 2
Retirement Budget:
  Food _________________
  Household _________________
  Transportation _________________
  Education _________________
  Clubs _________________
  Travel _________________
  etc _________________
  ____
  ____

Total Retirement Budget _________________

Step 3
Inflation-Factor: _________________
  (See Table 11)

Inflation-Adjusted Retirement Budget _________________
  (Multiply inflation-factor times total
  retirement budget)

Step 4
Retirement Income:
  Social security _________________
  Pension _________________
  Other _________________
Projected Retirement Income _________________

Step 5
Total Additional Yearly Income
Needed At Retirement _________________
  (step 3 minus step 4)

Step 6
Accumulated Savings or Investments Required
To Provide This Additional Income _________________
  (Divide step 5 by estimated return
  on savings or investments)

Step 7
Amount That Must Be Saved or Invested
Each Week Or Month To Accumulate Total
In Step 6 _________________
  (See Table 12)

Table 11

INFLATION FACTORS FOR USE ON THE RETIREMENT WORKSHEET

Years Until Retirement	Inflation Factors					
	3%	4%	5%	6%	7%	8%
5	1.16	1.22	1.28	1.34	1.40	1.47
10	1.34	1.48	1.63	1.79	1.97	2.16
15	1.56	1.80	2.08	2.40	2.76	3.17
20	1.81	2.19	2.65	3.21	3.87	4.66
25	2.09	2.67	3.39	4.29	5.43	6.85
30	2.43	3.24	4.32	5.74	7.61	10.06

Table 12

SAVING TO BUILD A RETIREMENT NEST EGG

Desired IRA Amount	Weekly Savings Required	Monthly Savings Required	For This Many Yrs
$ 50,000	27.70	119.64	15
	15.12	65.30	20
	8.65	37.37	25
	5.08	21.94	30
$100,000	30.23	130.60	20
	17.30	74.74	25
	10.16	43.87	30
	6.05	26.12	35
$200,000	34.61	149.49	25
	20.31	87.75	30
	12.09	52.24	35
	7.26	31.36	40
$300,000	30.47	131.62	30
	18.14	78.36	35
	10.89	47.05	40
$400,000	24.19	104.49	35
	14.52	62.73	40
$500,000	30.24	130.62	35
	18.15	78.41	40

Based on 10% annual interest, compounded monthly, in an IRA. Deposits made at the beginning of each week or month.

Table 13

HOW LONG A RETIREMENT NEST EGG WILL LAST

Accumulated Funds	Annual Withdrawal For Fund To Last 9 Yrs	Annual Withdrawal For Fund To Last 14 Yrs
$ 50,000	$ 8,000	$ 6,000
$100,000	$16,000	$12,000
$150,000	$24,000	$18,000
$200,000	$32,000	$24,000
$250,000	$40,000	$30,000
$300,000	$48,000	$36,000
$350,000	$56,000	$42,000
$400,000	$64,000	$48,000
$450,000	$72,000	$54,000
$500,000	$80,000	$60,000

Based on after-tax fund earnings of 8% annually. Actual time fund lasts will vary, depending on actual growth rates, withdrawal rates, and taxes.

IN
OUT

$$4$$

A Family Budget Plan

With any luck, you may have all the money needed to pay for your family's wants when the bills are due. Of course, any former *Boomerang* Player can tell you about luck. Or, if you prefer not to leave such matters to chance, you can plan your future spending and income. This allows scheduling of goals to keep pace with the family checkbook. But there is more at stake here than avoiding overdrafts. You need a plan to get the things you want and to make them more than just words on a wish list.

In theory at least, money flows two ways: in and out. This is good news if you have been watching your money go out lately. This "outflow" is money that has been spent for family wants or it should have been. And the "inflow" is money earned or collected that has come in to pay for them.

Naturally, the inflow is the one that seems to drip while the outflow rushes in a whirlpool as if the plug has been pulled on the kitchen sink. But those incoming drops can accumulate with time, and most of us have learned not to pull the plug on the outflow. Planning is simply getting these future money flows in balance. Since you must pay for wishes when they are received—or at least in installments—you need to break down their cost according to how and when in the year you expect to pay for them. It is not enough to know their price. You must have the money at the checkout counter. Otherwise, your family's favorite choices will be placed back on the shelf while you explain to the store manager why you can't pay for them just now.

Where should you begin planning? Right now, a little voice may be telling you to begin by adding up income first. This little voice is your conservative conscience. Whatever you do, don't listen to him. He is afraid of his shadow, let alone any new ideas that appear risky. If starting with inflow seems prudent, no doubt you are concerned about living within your income. Translated, this means the quickest way down the financial drain is to spend more than you earn. And it's true. But by adding up future income first to limit spending to it, you also limit family wants. Worse, you miss the view of how income is affecting them. The best place to begin is with spending—your future outflow. When finished, you will have matched the money going out with the money coming in. But in the process, you will discover how much more income is needed to obtain family goals.

Estimating Future Outflow

Now that it's settled on where to start, pull out the family's wish list—those selections that everyone bargained brilliantly for at the council. To make a plan to obtain them, simply write each want and its cost under the month when you expect to pay for it. Some choices will require monthly payments. Others may call for a one–time payment. By breaking down the cost of each item into the months, you will see the timing of future money outflow. In turn, this gives you time to figure out how to come up with the money. Before you start worrying about which bank to rob, refine your cost estimates. Maybe some of those prices for family choices are too high, considering your wheeler-dealer skills. There is no sense in dynamiting the bank vault if a loan is all that is needed. Then again, some prices may be set too low, considering inflation and changes already built-in to your family's future spending. Planning is where all of these things are taken into account.

Many necessities will follow last year's payment pattern. The heating bill goes up when it gets cold, insurance premiums are due at the same lousy time, and Uncle Sam gets his share of the money on April 15, unless your family is on the pay-early program. You can make monthly cost estimates for the coming year by looking at last year's spending. Then adjust for changes that can reasonably be predicted and possibly, for inflation.

For new choices on your list, put their cost into the coming months when the money will be paid out for them. The cost of a new bedroom set may belong in April's spending column. Bills from a summer vacation should arrive in August and September. Or the new car you hope to buy may require a down payment in August and monthly installments for the rest of the year.

Proceed down your family's list of wants and include all of them on your plan, just as if you had good sense and money to burn. Besides seeing how you might spend money if you were rich, there is a method to this madness, as you will discover later. In the meantime, enjoy your wealth.

Slowing Down Money Outflow

Money buys less during periods of inflation. This means you will need more inflow just to stay even—unless you are going to fight inflation. Then you can let everyone else get poorer while you, shrewd want–buyer that you are, find the bargains. Don't accept inflation without a fight. Time purchases to obtain the best buys, look for ways to conserve on energy in your home and automobiles, and don't be satisfied with last year's prices. You can get even lower prices by shopping around.

Take advantage of "loss leaders," the items a store advertises at low prices just to attract customers. When you see these—and you see them every week of the year—stock up on bargains and save money by avoiding higher prices later on. My wife would not know a loss leader if the store manager hit her over the head with one. This is because she doesn't recognize the term "loss leader." But she does know that our newspaper is full of ads each week that offer big savings on everything from toothpaste to fruit cocktail or whatever else happens to be on sale at the store where she shops. Depending on her stocks at home and the bargains selling at fire-sale prices, she often buys in case lots. Right now, our family has enough toothpaste to keep the entire neighborhood free of cavities for a year. Is my wife wise for buying in such large quantities? Yes. Am I smart for forgetting to bring along toothpaste on my last business trip and paying twice the price for a smaller tube? Don't ask.

Whatever you do, don't buy on impulse. If you remember the items displayed near the checkout counter at the supermarket, you already know about impulse buying. In this strategic location in the store are all the wonderful things that people don't need, but that are likely to be bought anyway. Take fresh donuts, for instance. My grocer always puts these treats near the checkout stand where shoppers can stand in line and see, smell, and crave them, while they wait. My impulse is to buy all the donuts in the store. But I don't. They are not on my want list. On the contrary, one of my goals this year is to avoid looking like the "Goodyear Blimp." To avoid impulse buying, I write at the top of my shopping list: "No donuts, Fatso." You may prefer more subtle reminders, but plan shopping trips to buy what you intend to buy and nothing more.

Some of my macho friends figure that looking for loss leaders, avoiding impulse buying, and hunting for bargains is sissy stuff reserved for women. This probably explains why they are fleeced out of their money so easily when buying tractors, tools, hardware, trucks, and other macho items. As it happens, bargains are everywhere, not just the supermarket. And buying them is not a practice reserved strictly for women, though I suspect they often do a better job of it than men do. If you can explain the logic of men in the family ignoring smart shopping practices while women carry the burden of stretching the family dollar, I'd like to hear it. In the meantime, make certain everyone in the family looks for loss leaders, never buys on impulse, and hunts for bargains ruthlessly.

Sure, your family will pay more for some wants. But these increases can be offset with bargains on other things. Remember that the price you pay is unique. By selecting when and where to buy your family choices, and the method to pay for them, you have considerable influence in the marketplace. Maybe it's time to use your clout.

When drafting this plan, adjust estimates for those costs expected to increase. If something on the list can be bought for less, make an estimate for the amount you expect to pay. You won't make your family's plan inflation–proof this way, but then, you won't be kidding yourself either. Best of all, you won't put another nickel in the inflation meter for the rest of us to worry about.

Count on changes in spending. A new car to replace a worn-out gas guzzler should lower spending for gas and repairs. On second thought, if your teenager's new girlfriend lives in the next county and he drives the family car, figure more gas, not less. But either way, changes affect money outflow. Your family is a year down the road from last year's spending. Think about the changes that have occurred since then. How will these alter your family's spending plans? You may not pay for braces for the children's teeth, as you did last year. On the other hand, you could wind up buying formals for the school prom next year. Will your kids mention prom formals at the family council? Not a chance. They'll get their favorite wishes at the top of the family's list and announce the need for formals two days before the prom. Even so, some of life's little surprises can be anticipated by reflecting on the year ahead. Who knows? You might discover an old loan that will be paid off in the middle of the coming year, leaving extra dollars for other things—like formals for the school prom.

It's a virtual certainty that family spending for the coming year won't follow exactly last year's spending patterns. People know this instinctively, yet many of them make a plan that could pass for a carbon copy of last year's spending. Why live in the past? You'll do better looking ahead. If you are one of those people who has trouble seeing beyond next week, pull out a calendar for the coming months and look at the dates in your future. It's amazing how many things in life are predictable, if you stop to think about them. Whether your family is expecting twins or a litter of pups, include the new arrivals in your plan. Just remember to adjust for likely occurrences, and not far-out possibilities.

As a child, you had an allowance or wished you did. Now that you are grown up, you pay taxes. With this kind of progress, everyone knows that the kids have a better deal. But even if you can't escape paying taxes, take a lesson from the children and award yourself an allowance. All family members need some money of their own to spend. The money that is set aside for each member's allowance should be spent as Mom, Dad, or Spot wants to spend it—no questions asked. This makes a plan flexible. It also provides for another desire: unplanned spending. Ironically, this is something that can be planned. Allowance money is special. It can buy grape sodas or bubble gum for the younger crowd. Or, for older kids like you, it might be the money for a luncheon with a friend or megabucks for scuba gear, depending on your interests and the amont of your allowance. If living with a plan is new to your family members, provide some extra room for adjustment by increasing the size of their allowances.

Estimating Future Inflow

Complete the inflow portion of your plan in the same way that you completed the spending part: use last year's income as a guide and adjust for any expected changes. But don't get carried away. If you are definitely scheduled for an increase in pay, include the money. On the other hand, if you bet on Leadfoot at 30 to 1 odds to win in the third race, don't include the expected windfall in your family's new plan.

Adjusting Money Flows

After totaling everything, compare the money flows for the year. If, by some oddity, you have more inflow that outflow, decide what to do with the excess money. Few people find themselves in this position, but if you are one of them, expand your wish list. Or, buy some choices at a faster pace. Whether you plan to save, spend, or give away this excess money, include it on your plan. Then write a letter telling the rest of us how you managed to get in this predicament in the first place. We'd be interested to know.

If your plan has more money going out than is coming in for the year, you need to make some adjustments. Unless Uncle Harry dies and leaves you a bundle of cash (worse odds than Leadfood winning), you must find more inflow or reduce outflow. Otherwise, some family choices may have to be postponed, unless you come up with something brilliant for your plan. One way or another, the money flows must balance for the year. Since your family's wish list is at stake, drag out some of that cleverness you had when you were young and single. Your spouse didn't marry you just for your good looks.

Making The Inflow Faucet Drip Faster

A lot of things can add to money inflow. Part-time jobs for the kids, renting the basement, selling arts and crafts, or moonlighting with a second job can do it. Or, pretend your family is moving and dig out those old items that no one cares to own any longer. Have a sale. The result? More inflow. What about the money loaned to a friend or relative that you never expect to see again? Collecting this debt means more dollars to apply toward your wants. Selling something that is financed can improve both inflow and outflow at the same time by providing the cash to pay off a loan with additional money left over. The options are endless. Just make certain your plans are carried out if you intend to base family wants on them.

It's no secret that borrowing can improve the money coming in. In fact, a loan can do wonders for inflow. Unfortunately, the money must be paid back—a provision that lenders regard fondly, and one that can play havoc with your family's money outflow. If you plan to enhance inflow with debt, use it wisely. Among other things, this means not having too much of it. How much is too much? One good rule of thumb says don't have more than twenty percent of your income going to make payments on debts, not counting a mortgage. So, derive a figure that represents twenty percent of your take-home pay. Then add up current payments on debt to see how you fit the rule. Don't try improving inflow with debt, if you already have too much of it. If there is room for additional debt, weigh the cost of it—interest— against the value of obtaining some things sooner or waiting for them. Then decide. If borrowing is included on the inflow side of a plan, include paying it back on the outflow side.

Restricting Outflow

Check your cost estimates again. Have you included family wants at the best price that can be reasonably expected? If not, if you have been overly cautious with estimates, revise them. The same washer and dryer that costs eight hundred dollars at the store should not be projected to cost a thousand dollars on your plan. After all, this is not a budget for some government agency. Don't pad cost estimates with extra dollars to provide a margin of safety. Bureaucrats do this to avoid overspending their budget and explaining the embarrassment to their boss. This strategy works when playing with someone else's money. But it is your dollars at stake. Make cost estimates as accurate as possible. Then challenge everyone in the family to stick to them. If something can be purchased at a lower price, why deprive your family of other goals by inflating cost estimates?

Some wants come brand new, right out of the box. Yet people could obtain the same item for less money by purchasing second-hand. Will they do it? Sometimes. But more often than not, they will bypass opportunities to buy the used item and pick the new one. Now it's true that some things should not be bought used. I wouldn't buy used toothpaste, for example. But people think nothing of buying a home previously owned or a car that has been "road-tested." With our choices falling into these two groups, it is better to begin with the idea of buying used items, then rule out the choices that should come new. This insures that some bargains aren't overlooked. If you buy an item for enjoyment, some previously owned choices will provide the same effect as a new item. My youngest son doesn't care if he rides a new tricycle. He cares only that he rides a tricycle. Review your wish list again to see if he knows something that you have forgotten.

There are plenty of ways to reduce the cost of family desires. Maybe you can trade something, such as time or skills, for a favorite choice, rather than buy it. Let's say, for example, that a double garage is high on your wish list this year. It can easily cost a lot of money these days. But you can cut the price down to size by building the garage yourself, if you have the time and talent to do it. If not, find a builder who will trade his skills for the type of work you do. Finding ways to get the bargains and reduce the cost of a family wish list is worth more than you might think.

Yes, but what you really need, what we all need, is more income. I remember my father telling me as a youngster that our family would be rich if he earned ten thousand dollars a year. Later, when he earned this amount and more, we were far from wealthy. Having learned this lesson early in life, I graduated from college with the acute foresight of knowing that a certain income would put me on easy street. It didn't. Somewhere in the human mind is a light bulb that illuminates to show us that the key to solving all of our problems is more income, and merely breathing switches on that bulb.

Granted, with more income, you could skip the indignity of haggling in the marketplace to save a few dollars on the cost of things. But saving money on costs can yield a better return than earning the extra money. For example, if you save twenty dollars on the cost of say, parking fees, this money can be applied toward other desires. Conversely, if you should extract a twenty dollar pay raise from your cheapskate boss, you may keep only fifty cents of each additional dollar earned after income taxes. I don't know about you, but I would rather save. Fortunately, the government hasn't figured out how to tax the dollars saved on parking fees yet.

Contrary to popular notion, necessities are not sacred. Admittedly, it is difficult to cut their cost because necessities often involve fixed obligations. But that is no reason to look the other way. A mortgage payment that cramps your lifestyle may warrant a change of address for one that doesn't strain the family finances. If you are in this position, sell your home and move into another, where the payments are less burdensome. Similarly, if payments on a new car or other possession have your family strapped for cash and freedom, sell them. Why should possessions live better than you do? If pride of ownership is worth sacrificing some of the little things in life like freedom from creditors and more choice spending, by all means, keep the possessions. But it's bad arithmetic to put gas in a car that eats better than you do. And watching the bulk of a paycheck go to pay off old debts doesn't add up either. In this case, it is time to get rid of those freeloading possessions and start taking care of family goals. Remember, you do have options. It is simply a matter of choice.

Of course, the really impossible costs to cut are utility bills, right? While you're figuring out ingenious ways to lower the cost of electricity, water, or heat, the public utility is out begging for a rate increase. It happens every time. You load up on home insulation. You buy the special light bulbs that save electricity and will outlive most cats. And then, just when you have slashed the cost of utilities, the company raises their rates. But you will counter this move with even more conservation and beat the system, true or false? Well, true, the cost of utility bills can be cut, and false, you won't, if you don't get down there and raise cane about any more rate increases. It is amazing how many dollars are spent each year on insulation, storm windows, and other energy or resource saving devices while few people stand up to be heard at public hearings held on rate increases. Anything that affects the cost of your family wish list deserves attention. Why should you care if the cost of electricity, city services, or heating oil goes up? You should care because one way or another these increases take away dollars to buy other things. Instead of the silent majority, most of us need to become part of a new vocal majority.

As it happens, hundreds of ways are available to reduce the cost of utilities. The easier things, like turning off the lights or heat when you don't need them are not earth-shattering, but they can work to cut the dollar amount of utility bills. Or, take more drastic measures as a friend of mine did. When he decided his heating bill was too high, he casually mentioned to the utility company that he wasn't going to pay any more of their bills. The same day his service was terminated. Also the same day, his wood-burning stove started heating his home at a fraction of the cost he was paying before. In short, he combined another want, family outings in the woods, with his warm-and-cozy goal. This way his family enjoys the wonders of the forest while gathering firewood for their home. The lesson here is don't make any casual remarks about not paying your utility bills, and if you do, have an alternative ready. In the meantime, figure that necessities like utilities deserve the same attention as the rest of your choices when it comes to cutting costs.

If All Else Fails

If the last nickel has been squeezed from the cost of everything and your plan still isn't balanced, say hello to truth or consequences. If it is true that your plan isn't balanced, here are the consequences: you must temporarily postpone some choices on your family's wish list. Sad, but true. Naturally, the smart thing is to postpone the least important wants first. (Not for nothing did you decide priorities!) Needless to say, it is painful to watch while some goals fall by the wayside and are removed from your plan for the coming year. But if you don't know which choices are temporarily delayed and keep a record of them, you will have no idea how much additional income is required to get them. Granted, the easy way out is to begin a plan by adding up income first, then limit spending to it. This avoids the pain of seeing some goals delayed. The logic is that you won't miss what you don't know about. On the other hand, you won't get it either. To obtain those postponed items, you need to know how much additional inflow is required in order to come up with the money. This information can be useful later.

When swinging the budget ax to balance your plan, don't chop off the allowances of family members. Trim them, if necessary, but don't eliminate them. Otherwise, your whole plan could be lost because of family resistance if you try to force everyone to live with a budget that is too rigid. Now, far be it from me to tell you to put off acquiring your favorite golf clubs. But it is better to delay these than whack away at allowances to the point where a plan is inflexible.

All Things Equal

When all is said and done, your family's plan must balance. This means the total amount of money to be received for the year is the same as the amount going out. Never mind that the money-flows during the months are not balanced. Just make certain the yearly totals are the same—exactly. Close counts only when you are playing horseshoes or throwing hand grenades.

Fine-Tuning A Plan

Now, if this balancing act is managed and everything goes according to plan, there is a good chance your family will starve in March and have money to throw away in August. Some months will have more money flowing out than is flowing in and vice versa. One way to deal with this problem is to spread excess spending in some months over the course of the year.

My wife and I once bought an insurance policy for newlyweds, the kind that pays double if you accidentally shoot yourself in the foot and die. The glib salesman failed to mention that the annual premium came due on April 15. Thereafter, we scrambled to come up with the money each year for both insurance and taxes. After a few years of this nonsense, we decided to look for a solution. Canceling our policy was out of the question, since it had a cash value that we didn't want to forfeit. So we opened up a savings account, designated this one as our "insurance fund," and contributed a portion of the insurance premium to it each month. In the middle of April each year, we used the money accumulated in savings to pay the insurance premium. Now we scramble on April 15 strictly for Uncle Sam, which gives you some idea of how much we have learned since then.

Even so, you can do what we did. Simply open a new savings account, call it an insurance fund, and make monthly payments to it. When the premium comes due, withdraw from savings to pay it. With twelve months head start, you will have the money. With six month's jump on the due date, you will have at least half of it. And other spending can be spread out the same way. If you plan a summer vacation and the outflow to pay for it will occur all in one month, set up another savings account. Make this one a vacation fund and contribute a set amount to it each month. Besides having the money when it's time to leave on holiday, it is a good bet that you will enjoy this vacation even more, knowing that its cost has been taken care of in advance.

So here you are with thirty-seven savings accounts, ready to pay diligently to them, and yet the money flows still won't balance every month. A lawyer I know has the same problem. His paydays are far apart and few in between, which is to say, he doesn't receive his income regularly like most of us. To balance his money flows, he borrows during those months when expenses exceed income. Then, during the months when more dollars flow in than go out, he pays the money back. Simple. What's more, he never sees his banker for a loan to even out the money flows. Instead, he borrows from an established savings account where he has money stashed for just such purposes. True, he loses interest on his savings when borrowing, but he considers this a small price to pay for not having to balance the money flows each month. If you are one of those people who tap savings only in case of emergencies, earthquakes, or similar disasters, fine. See a loan officer. Or match the money flows for each month on your plan.

All Done?

As the saying goes, the opera is not over until the fat lady sings. The same holds true for your family's money plan. It is not complete until the money flows for the year are balanced. You can spread out spending over the calendar year or borrow from savings to avoid going from feast to famine during the months of the year. Once this has been accomplished, your plan is complete. Go ahead and sing.

Revisions

Unless you lead a charmed life, you will return later to make some adjustments and revisions to your plan. Why? Because no one can predict the future with certainty. You may be awarded a huge increase in utility bills. Uncle Harry may come through with an inheritance. Who knows? The only sure thing that can be counted on is change. And when changes come along, some adjustments will be necessary to your plan. This keeps it up–to–date and shows how major changes affect your family's wants. With timely information, adjustments can be made in the plan to keep on track toward your goals. In the meantime, celebrate. You have a plan. It's time to collect from friends who bet that you'd never have a budget.

Table 14

SUGGESTIONS FOR A FAMILY MONEY PLAN

Always set up allowances in your plan for all family members. This improves the odds against finding the budget in the garbage later on. And everyone receives some freedom to spend money as they alone intend.

Would you like a letter from the credit card people stating that old balances have been wiped out to provide a fresh start? While waiting for this to happen, include credit card balances along with other debts as a goal on your plan, "Getting Out of Debt." Then you can make it happen by paying off credit card balances.

Include savings on your plan. The secret to a successful savings program is a method that contributes to it regularly without fail. A payroll savings plan at work can do it. Or, set up monthly payments to a savings account, and pay yourself first at the beginning of each month.

When looking for ways to improve money inflow, include only those methods that are virtually certain to work in the coming year.

To support your church or favorite charity, make regular contributions and include them on your plan. Worthy causes need planning too. And regular support instead of random donations can be a double help.

Don't allow mortgage payments, car payments, and outstanding debts to become so large that other spending is reduced to chicken feed. If you are in this position starting out, find ways to reduce fixed obligations. Otherwise, you will begin to think that you are working for someone else's benefit—which you are!

Insurance premiums may not be due monthly unless you have elected to pay them that way. By using a savings account designated as an "insurance fund," monthly payments can be made to the account that will earn interest, instead of electing monthly payments from the insuror and paying interest.

Table 15

HOW TO MAKE A FAMILY MONEY PLAN

---

1. Put all family goals on your plan by writing their cost under the months when you expect to pay for them.

2. Include future income amounts under the months when the money will be received.

3. Add the yearly money inflows and outflows to determine if they balance. They won't, but add them anyway. This shows how many adjustments need to be made to get a balance.

4. Look for ways to increase money inflow and adjust your plan for those methods that will work this coming year.

5. Find possible ways to reduce money outflow and adjust your plan accordingly.

6. If necessary, remove some family goals from your plan to balance the yearly money flows. Remove the least important goals first and keep a list of them.

7. Match the total yearly amount of money going out on your plan with the amount of money coming in for the year.

8. Make minor adjustments to your plan by spreading out spending so that inflows and outflows balance for each month, or nearly so.

9. For those months when the money flows won't balance, plan to borrow from savings when spending is more than inflow. Plan to pay the money back during those months when the reverse is true.

10. Revise your plan when major changes come along that make it outdated or unrealistic.

Table 16
THE FAMILY'S PLAN

OUTFLOW	JAN	FEB	MAR	APR	MAY	JUN	JUL	AUG	SEP	OCT	NOV	DEC	YEAR
warm & cozy													
lights at nite													
water on tap													
other utilities													
keeping the house													
protection													
mom													
dad													
kids													
car													
nest egg													
fun													
medic!													
gifts													
food													
clothes													
household													
new boat													
trips													
entertain													
vacation													
education													
investment													
golf clubs													
go cart													
kitchen remodel													
pay old debts													
TOTAL OUTFLOW													
INFLOW													
paycheck													
garage sale													
kids													
investments													
interest													
new loan													
miracles													
TOTAL INFLOW													

$$5$$

Improving Future Income

How much additional income would be needed to include all the postponed wants on your plan? Okay, so you are bound to get lucky sooner or later. But before answering the get-rich-quick ads, think about how much money it will take to buy the least important choice on your family's delayed list of goals. You don't need to inherit an oil well to get this one. Chances are, this last item is your personal favorite, considering the negotiating skills of the rest of the family at the council. And if there is any justice in this world, surely you will find a way to get it. A pay raise might provide the needed money, though you may have already counted on stretching your luck in the previous chapter. But there are other ways to obtain the money. Warm up your probing mind from those old detective days. You might use wheeler-dealer skills for buying low and selling high. Whether trading in stocks or bonds, used cars, or real estate, it's possible to increase inflow nicely by sticking with familiar investments. Or, if you are the smooth talker that everyone says you are, sell something and pocket the commissions to earn the extra money. Knowing the price of postponed wants, even the last one on the list, provides a target for future income. And any sharpshooter knows the advantage of a stationary target. While everyone else is convinced they need more income, you will know how much more is needed.

Your personal choices on the delayed list of goals don't carry much weight with the rest of the family. Everyone is more interested in their own favorites that have been put on the sideline. Strangely enough, this provides some common ground. If family members really want their favorite choices that have been postponed, they can pitch in and find ways to earn them. This situation can do wonders for everyone's enterprising nature. Former dependents in the family can turn into budding entrepreneurs overnight. Younger kids with no apparent talent for counting past their allowance can syndicate a deal that is the envy of the downtown business district. Stranger things have happened. Just be prepared for a few surprises along the way. Last year, the grade school principal called to complain that my daughter was acquiring all of the other kids' lunch money. It turned out that she was selling comic strip characters glued on posterboard, a novelty her peers regarded more highly than the school's food. Her enterprise was hastily channeled in new directions, but I was proud of her, nonetheless.

Naturally, the key to all of this creativity is everyone's favorite choices on temporary hold. But a family can pool ideas to make this brainstorming session a collective one. For instance, remember those interesting ways that your family received money last year? Can some of those earning activities be expanded to cash in on proven techniques? This kind of brainstorming affords side benefits, especially if made a family affair. Teamwork makes younger members feel a part of the process and gives them positive attitudes toward earning money. Moreover, they develop a sense of worth, something all of us could use in larger quantities. Besides, kids are enterprising by nature. You never know when one of them will come up with a great idea. In the meantime, what better way to teach them that money does not grow on trees?

If you sold Christmas cards door-to-door as a youngster, you probably did so to earn money to buy something. Back then, it may have been a sleeping bag or a basketball. But your interests have changed. Now you'd settle for a ranch style home with a jacuzzi, skylights, and a breakfast nook. Never mind that you'd trade the sleeping bag and a right arm to get it. The question is, are you going to sell Christmas cards door-to-door again to acquire this dream home? Not unless you plan on selling a lot of Christmas cards. A method of earning money is needed that matches your objective. Acquiring a dream home might call for trading up. You can trade a present home for another and pick up several thousand extra dollars in the deal. I've known people who kept trading this way until they obtained their goal. One young couple is well on their way to acquiring the home of their dreams using this technique. They frequently change residences, but with better results than if they sold Christmas cards door-to-door to earn the money. What if you don't own a home to trade up? Buy one. If you can't afford the down payment, find an owner who wants to sell, assume the mortgage on his home, and make a deal to finance the down payment with a second mortgage. This kind of financing happens every day. Obstacles can be overcome. Just remember to match earning methods with the family goals they are intended to obtain. This helps to insure that all the options come to mind.

Not all family wants are compatible. Sometimes we must choose between opposite attractions. But there are income solutions to those conflicting choices, if you look hard enough to find them. My friend Tom had just such a choice to make.

"I love my work," he told me. "But my company is leaving the area. My family doesn't want to move from the community, and I've got to decide what to do."

"Why not change jobs," I suggested.

"Where am I going to find another job like mine in this town," he asked.

Tom was right. He had a specialized job in electronics, not the sort of work found at the local filling station or anywhere in our small community for that matter. He could change careers, but I wasn't going to be the one to suggest it. Since his family didn't want to move, I was out of suggestions.

A few months later I saw Tom, and he was beaming with pleasure.

"What happened?" I asked, sensing that something had changed.

"I'm commuting to a new job," he grinned.

He wasn't kidding. Now, Tom commutes to work half way around the world every other month. Granted, his idea of commuting is different from most people's notion, but his goals are not. He works overseas one month and spends the next month entirely with his family. He admits that his schedule isn't for everyone, but he enjoys it. His family has kept their new home, the children are growing up with the same friends, and Tom has remained active in community affairs. Moreover, he is saving money from his higher salary as a step toward a new income goal: he plans to buy a small business in our community. When family goals seem impossible to resolve, that is the time to look for uncommon income solutions, the ones off the beaten path.

Yes, well, hooray for all those folks who like working overseas. Personally, you might consider any employment outside the city limits as foreign, unappealing, and the last thing you would ever do. So what does a family who likes apple pie and hometown America do to get their delayed choices? For starters, those extra dollars don't have to be earned all at once. The money can be earned in steps, in the same way that you accumulate savings. Night school or training seminars can provide the education needed to make a career change, a move up the job ladder, or success with investments. It can be one step. Starting a small business can be a step. Or even buying a rental property—it can be a step toward getting more of those family wants. If you need twenty thousand dollars of additional income per year, why not find the steps needed to earn it? How many rental houses would provide this amount? What kind of earnings could be expected from additional job training to advance to a higher-paying position? The step-by-step income plan will beat the get-rich-quick schemes every time.

Earning additional money one step at a time is not nearly as glamorous as investing. A television crew is not going to show up and film a documentary of your advance toward extra income one step at a time. Instead, they'll tape a story on some enchanting investment and put it on the screen next week just to show where everyone else is making a fortune. But what they won't mention is that most people earn far more over their lifetimes by working than they do by investing. In perspective, this means that the greatest opportunity for improving earnings comes not from investments, but from work. But this doesn't mean working blindly. When a housewife with interior decorating skills can earn more in a day or two than her husband might earn in a week at the factory, our economy is changing. Each day it is becoming more of a service economy. This translates into untold earning opportunities for people who can provide the services that others desire. If you haven't thought about climbing on this bandwagon, it's time you did. Don't allow the glamour of investments to take attention away from working more wisely and earning more for it.

True, you'll have to take some chances. To earn more income, particularly if family goals require substantial earnings to reach, you must take risks. This is different from gambling that you can beat the bus across the street. The kind of risks that should be taken are calculated, meaning the odds of earning and losing are known in advance. This allows weighing the risks against the potential rewards to see if the risks are worth taking. To improve income, don't shy away from risks.

But people do. And that is precisely why they forfeit income opportunity. Good old-fashioned security is what they often prefer, even if it is an illusion. Take job security, for instance. If people who work for the government can't be absolutely sure of having a job, how can anyone be sure? Yet everyday people pass up income opportunities to cling to job security. The boss can fire them tomorrow and they'll be out on the street, not looking for income opportunity, but for another secure job. If you have fallen into this trap, pull out by starting to take some calculated risks. Sure, you can lose by buying rental properties and having no tenants. You can also lose with safe investments in public utility bonds, too. But the expensive loss, the one you can't afford, is sitting on the sidelines, fearing risk. You won't improve income without taking some chances.

The best way to put the odds for income success in your favor is by finding an earning activity that you enjoy. It can be a hobby. Or it might be an idea from work. But whatever it is, your love for it is a big advantage over other earning activities that you might select. People who have a passion for their work, an idea, a venture, or an innovation always seem to fare better financially than the people who are passive about an earning source. For instance, take the model train buff who writes for a magazine. He first began with a love for his hobby. Later, he expanded it into an earning source. Or, what about the lady with the green thumb who can grow anything? People pay for her advice. But she began first by doing something she enjoyed. Even the inventor who earns millions from a gadget that makes life easier for the rest of us began with a love for tinkering with ideas. He may have thousands of inventions in his basement that are worthless, but he cherishes every one of them. People who enjoy financial success generally enjoy what they do. Discover what earning activities spur your motivation and pursue them. This provides the best advantage possible.

Too many people underestimate the value of doing what they enjoy to earn income. These are the folks who will keep a job that they detest, no matter what:

"I can't leave this job," a lady told me. "They pay me too well to leave."

Never mind that she hated the job.

A banker tells the same story, only with a different twist. He can't quit because his stature in the community is important to him, even though he dreads going to work each day.

Finding a job that you enjoy may require some trade-offs, perhaps even settling for less family wants at times, but the price is worth it. My roommate in college learned this lesson the hard way. He gave up an occupation he dearly loved—teaching history—for the lure of big dollars in the business world. He earned a handsome income, but he was miserable. Fortunately, he saw his mistake early. Today, he teaches history again and no one enjoys their job more than he enjoys teaching. He came back to his first love—history—and to the kids for whom he makes the subject come alive every day. True, his teaching salary is modest. But he has capitalized on his business experience and now earns additional income as a guest speaker, tapping his own unique talents and a desire for the subject he loves. Is he winning the money game? Bet the ancient pyramids on it.

Table 17

HOW TO MAKE AN INCOME PLAN

1. Begin with delayed family goals as targets for the income needed to reach them.

2. List past skills and experiences that are potential earning sources. If you know the hardware business, for example, don't be concerned that you don't have the money to buy a store or franchise. Just put your skill on the list.

3. Match earning methods with family goals desired. Look at all of the possibilities for earning each goal and write them down.

4. Look for uncommon earning sources. Lots of people have regular jobs. Find income ideas that are off the beaten path.

5. List the steps needed to reach an earning activity that will provide a desired income. For example, if a certain level of training is required for a particular job with the right income, list the necessary steps for getting in line for the job.

6. Take calculated risks. Determine the amount of money in savings or elsewhere that you are prepared to risk for improving earnings. When people feel angry at themselves for not taking a chance, it's too late to grab the opportunity. Prepare in advance for opportunity by setting aside risk capital.

7. List all the potential income activities that you enjoy. Don't keep working in a job or profession in which you feel trapped. Plan the steps to move toward another type of work that is enjoyable. This may require keeping a present job temporarily while getting the training to make a career change.

8. Examine the ideas that you have accumulated for earning additional income. Weigh each idea and the trade-offs it may require. Map out an income plan, then put it in action. Don't allow fear of risk to stop you.

9. Include your family in this process. Consider everyone's ideas and help your children find opportunities in which they can succeed as well.

6

Following Your Family's Budget Plan

Do you need an incentive to follow your plan? Try the knuckle smasher. Every time you start to get off course by spending too much, this little device raps you on the knuckles. It's a great reminder. A small mistake costs only a light tap. A major offense—well, let's just say you won't be tempted to do it again.

Seriously, your family's wants are all the incentive necessary. Besides, the knuckle smasher is make-believe. Even if it were real, everyone would know how you are doing with the family budget by looking at your bruised knuckles—hardly discreet. Keep a record of spending and you can be as smug as your friends about money matters. And you will have a more effective reminder. The knuckle smasher tells only that you are off course. A money record can show just how far off you really are with spending.

Some families can follow their plan simply by knowing they have one. There must be at least a dozen of these families in the world. Meanwhile, the rest of us need a way to keep track of spending and compare it with our plans. How? Notebooks, ledgers, cookie jars, envelopes, secret compartments, or a dozen different checking accounts have been known to work. If your trusty homespun method is good enough to hold you to a plan, it is good enough to keep. The important thing is that it works and you are comfortable with it. Don't change an old method for a fancy new one when you have the tried and true. However, if you don't have a way to account for spending, a money record is necessary.

If the idea of recording family spending doesn't thrill you, join the crowd. Most of us would rather be shot first. But you can take some small comfort in knowing that the rest of the world is going to all this trouble for the wrong reason. The world does not need more paperwork. And you are not in the money game for the record–keeping. You are in it for your family's wants. This is why any money record should concern itself primarily with tracking family spending to get them. If it manages to impress the IRS at the same time by accumulating your tax deductions, fine. But family goals should not play second fiddle to tax considerations. If your money record keeps track of everything from the family history to what you had for dinner last Thursday, throw it out. You don't need distractions from goals.

In this age of electronic wizardry and home computers, the best money record may yet be a homemade version like the one I saw the other day. This homespun could dazzle the socks off a microchip for convenience. It folds neatly in the front of a checkbook and replaces the register where written checks are recorded. Instead of one column for spending, this one has a column for each family want. The couple who owns this gem records their spending under the appropriate column as they write checks. This allows them to keep track of their account balance and favorite choices at the same time. Granted, it doesn't keep track of where they hid their will or insurance policies. But it tracks their wants like a bloodhound, which was the idea in the first place. (See page 73.)

Setting Up The Money Machinery

When you spend, you generally pay cash, write a check, or use a credit card. We don't barter much anymore, though I'm told we should. Even so, there are other ways to spend the family's money as any third-grader who has accepted magazine subscriptions over the phone knows. Lay-away slips, mail orders, catalog phone orders, IOUs, and charge accounts are just a few of the modern inventions to pull the plug on the outflow. One of the first things a family should do is to set up procedures for spending. It doesn't make any different whether you use cash, checks, or credit cards, or even a combination of these. What matters is that you decide in advance the methods of spending

Table 18
YE OLE HOMESPUN CHECKING ACCOUNT RECORD

PLANS

Inflow	Date	Description	Ck#	Amt.	Bal.	Food	Clothes	Mom	Dad	Kids	House-hold	Car	Protec-tion	Educa-tion	Savings	Major Wants	Taxes	Invest-ments	Charge Pymts	Unplan Spendg

your family will use. This provides a fair chance of controlling the actual outflow to follow your plan. You don't need one family member out signing charge tickets at the store while everyone else is watching their checks, cash, or allowance money like a hawk.

Believe it or not, bank accounts can be set up to work in your favor. Payroll deductions or automatic withdrawals from your checking account can deposit money regularly in savings or investments. Once the money has been subtracted from your account, you won't have it to spend in other ways. For some people, this type of forced savings is the only method that works.

If investment monies routinely flow in and out of your family's finances, keep them in separate accounts. Otherwise, you can spend months nursing along a few shares of stock to earn a profit, only to sell them and find that the money earned has vanished for some worthy cause, like new tile for the bathroom. Put investment funds in separate accounts that pay interest when they are not reinvested immediately. And keep them there, unless you like the idea of paying tax on the bathroom tile.

Allowances should be paid regularly to family members from a checking account, not savings. This establishes a routine that everyone can rely on and avoids pulling the money helter-skelter from wherever it might be available. Besides, the community has a big stake in those allowances. Libraries must collect overdue book fines, the school play can't go on until your child pays her costume fee, and the computer games downtown will pop their circuits without a steady intake of quarters. Since life as everyone knows it cannot continue in your community without your family's allowances, you might as well make allowance day a predictable event.

With these kind of advance preparations adjusted to fit your family's lifestyle, you can make the money machinery help control spending and get the most out of your financial resources.

The friendly world of banking and credit is designed with your comfort in mind. And heaven forbid that you should have any trouble spending money. The financial folks will fall all over themselves to insure that you spend with the greatest of ease and convenience. No longer do you need to run the risk of being insulted by some rash clerk at the store over cashing a check. No clerk in his right mind is going to challenge your guaranteed check card. If you don't relish the thought of facing a stone-cold loan officer, why do it? Automatic overdrafts can lend the money. And if you should die, not to worry;

the credit card people will probably send you a new card anyway. Naturally, all this convenience has nothing whatever to do with controlling your family's spending. This is reason enough to cut out those frills that are not needed. Chances are, you never asked for some of them anyway. Take an inventory of money services that are excess baggage. Our family once had two checking accounts, the apparent benefit of which was to demonstrate an uncanny ability to keep both of them overdrawn at the same time. When we closed one account, the bank's computer sent a letter expressing deep regret. Make no mistake about who is concerned with controlling your spending. If you don't take charge, no one else will.

A handful of credit cards and multiple checking accounts doesn't always spell doom. If your family prefers two checking accounts, fine. Just make certain they serve a worthwhile purpose and enhance your ability to control spending rather than detract from it. One account might be used to pay the mortgage or rent payment each month. By doing so, you are less likely to forget these payments. Other types of spending can be separated with multiple checking accounts in the same way. Admittedly, this strategy isn't for everyone, but some people swear by it. I recommend it for people who enjoy solving puzzles, like bank statements. An easier approach, one I prefer, is designating a credit card to handle a specific type of spending. Travel and entertainment spending can be kept separate by charging on one card. If you frequently pay for business items that are reimbursed by your office, another card designated for this purpose can help separate your business and domestic life. Just make sure all those checking accounts or credit cards are controlled. Remember, financial services are designed with your convenience in mind, until you can't pay the bills. After that, there is nothing convenient about them.

Controlling Outflow

Writing a check is the same as handing over the money. Maybe it doesn't feel the same, but as surely as the sun comes up, your check will find its way back to your bank account. You can stand in the middle of the Yazoo River, write a check, hand it to someone, and invariably, it will arrive home before you do. Rarely will it become lost along the way, and almost never will it subtract money from someone else's account. With this kind of luck, you hand over the dollars every time you sign a check.

So why do people prefer writing checks over passing out the currency? True, checks are safer and muggers prefer cash. But another reason, one seldom admitted, is that writing checks is less painful than paying out the greenbacks. We don't feel the immediate sense of loss that we do when parting with the cash. Banks are reluctant to strap people in chairs and make them watch while money is subtracted from their accounts. If they did, the folks who survived the trauma would spend less. Since writing checks can be like putting on a blindfold, ask for dollar signs printed on your checks rather than some serene landscape where the deer and antelope play. This can help restore some of that old feeling for the value of a dollar, which is getting harder to remember these days. The more you value your family's money, the more value you will demand when parting with it.

Every time you spend money, you buy something. Pay a parking ticket and you donate to city hall. Never mind that the donation was unplanned. If you decide not to pay a ticket, the judge won't care if you planned to spend the money or not. Hardly a day goes by that we don't shell out money for some unplanned reason. This kind of spending is a cinch. But remembering those planned desires is not as easy. Unless these goals are kept in sight on a money record, you won't remember them. Simply transfer the monthly amounts on your plan to your record. The total of these is your spending limit for the month. When paying by check or cash, write down the purchase under the appropriate family choice. Then, as you record actual spending, compare it with planned amounts to see how you are doing. What could be more simple?

Credit Cards

If you prefer the convenience of credit cards, remember two things: first, you are spending cash and second, you will have to pay cash later. Convenience is worthwhile. Using credit cards to avoid facing family finances is not. When you spend by credit card, the flimsy customer copy becomes as important as your checkbook register. By no small coincidence, these receipts are easily lost and will flutter away in the slightest breeze. Family members who can't produce a customer copy should be able to prove they chased it no less than five miles in good faith. The last thing needed is to find out next month that someone in the family tried to buy out a store chain on credit this month. As charges are made, write them on a money record from the customer copies. If you want to keep credit card charges separate from checkbook spending, fine. Use a separate record. But however you choose to do it, compare actual spending with planned amounts to see how you are doing.

Why not record charges when writing the check to pay the card statement? By doing so, you could divide the payment into spending types and complete the task of recording them all at once. Meanwhile, you and Spot can sit on the front porch and wait for your statements to arrive. When the postman arrives with them, you may be the one doing the howling. So much for control. In short, you can't afford to wait a month for statements. By then, your family's spending will be ancient history. More timely information is needed if you expect to track spending to obtain family wants.

There's one hitch. By recording charges as they are made, you don't need to record them again when paying the card statements. When paying a credit card statement, do *not* write the payment in your record. If you forget and record these payments, you will be double counting your spending. And you can do without that kind of excitement at the end of the month.

Do you need a loan? Don't pay off the total balance due on a credit card statement and you will have one. It's easy and convenient. Also, expensive. This no-hassle borrowing usually costs around 18 to 21 percent interest. But you didn't plan to borrow money at these rates. (Who does?) Nor did you plan to borrow on your credit card. This is all the more reason to avoid credit card borrowing like the plague. Borrow money this way and you will need to record the interest charges in your money record. If this isn't enough to discourage you, try thinking about trading family wants for the privilege of paying interest.

Checking Inflow

The money that comes in should be recorded on your money record. Wonderful. That's all you need—something else to record. After all, who has trouble watching their inflow? Most of us do it instinctively, like breathing. If you doubt this, ask the postal clerks how many queries they receive from people whose paychecks are late. On the other hand, when was the last time you called about a lost check sent to someone else. Even so, include a place for inflow on your money record. It is not likely that you will forget those amounts due in your favor. But by listing the money received, you can compare it with planned amounts to make sure the inflow is dripping steadily as it should be. When money is received, write down where it is coming from—paycheck deposits, investment income, interest, or small miracles, like the money a relative owes you. This makes the detective work easier next year when trying to see how your family became so rich.

Are You On Track?

During the month you can compare actual spending with planned amounts to check progress toward family goals. At the end of the month, add up the total spent to see if your family spending stayed with the planned limit. Rarely, if ever, will actual spending be exactly as planned. Instead, you will either spend more or less than planned. Amazingly, this over or under spending doesn't mean anything until you know why. Say, for instance, you overspent on food last month. Despite what husbands and other budget experts might think, this means nothing. Maybe this overspending has converted a once-bare pantry into a food supply that will last well into next month, assuming your relatives don't visit. In this case, you may spend less money next month. Conversely, a big savings in the food budget is not always cause for celebration.

A few years ago, our family bought a steer from a farmer and had it processed into steaks, roasts, and other cuts of beef. We shared the costs with another family and split the beef. Accustomed as we were to buying beef this way, our friends were not. At first, they marveled at the cost savings over the supermarket price per pound, gleeful at the extra money in their budget. Unfortunately, they carried the celebration too far. Barbecues and steak dinners were suddenly standard meals at their home, and they entertained dinner guests twice as often as before. What began as a great savings in their food budget later turned out to be more expensive than if they had continued buying the higher priced beef at the store. Don't get nearsighted at the end of the month when comparing actual spending with planned amounts.

But knowing when your spending is getting off course is a big advantage. It allows for corrections to get back on course. If excess spending on food means saving money on next month's food budget, fine. If not, you just traded off some family wants. Sooner or later, you will have to bump some items off your plan to make room for higher food spending. But you do have options. Find the least important goals on your plan that add up to the amount of this excess spending. If you value these goals more than eating well, scrimp on food next month to make up for the excess spending. In this case, you choose to eat less to keep those other wants. And that is a choice you would not have without keeping track of spending. More often, people forfeit family goals and don't recognize that they have traded them off. Obviously, knowing your options in time to take advantage of them is worthwhile.

Anytime actual spending is exactly the way it was planned, put a notch on your six-shooter. And check to see if there is a full moon. With this kind of luck, you ought to go bowling or do whatever else you do. Almost never will actual spending follow your plan. Difficulties and new opportunities make it impossible to follow exactly. A plan covers a complete year. Along the way, adjustments must be made to the ebb and flow of changing events. By keeping track of spending, you can make small changes to stay on course toward family goals, adjusting to new realities. This is expected. But when events affect your plan in a major way, it's time to revise.

Your plan is not cast in stone. It must be flexible to adjust to current events. Revising a plan puts remaining goals in perspective again. You may need to delay another want temporarily, but at least you will have a plan for getting the rest of them. Maybe actual inflow isn't coming in as planned. Revise. Maybe the cost of some family choices is higher than first projected. Revise again. If a new opportunity comes along, don't pass it up simply because it is not on the plan. Check to see the effects on other goals if this opportunity is taken.

Say, for instance, your neighbor has been transferred to a new job in the Sahara desert and he must sell his boat. And you, generous soul, can take it off his hands for a thousand dollars. Are you going to pass up this opportunity because it is not on your plan? Of course not. You are going to buy this boat because it is worth maybe two thousand dollars minimum. Then you will promise to write. That's what you are going to do. But what you should do is figure out the family goals that will be given up by purchasing this boat, which is different from buying first and rationalizing your purchase later. If the boat still looks attractive after everyone in the family knows what goals will be waylaided, buy it. Skip any similar deals that can't wait for your review. If those new opportunities that come along are worthwhile, they can stand the test of weighing them against other goals to see how they stack up.

All too often, people who start a budget soon get bogged down in the numbers. They look at the amounts overspent in one place or another and worry about them until the original reason for following a plan is lost. Don't make this common mistake of getting bogged down with too much emphasis on record–keeping. And don't measure success entirely by whether or not your family spending stayed within a planned limit. Last year our family spent much more than we had planned on education. Was our budget a success? Absolutely. We obtained the majority of our goals in spite of this overspending. If we had despaired at the extra cost of school tuition for the kids and seminars, we might not have succeeded nearly so well with our overall budget. Remember, the whole idea is to get your family's wants. That requires looking ahead, not dwelling on the past.

Table 19

SUGGESTIONS FOR FOLLOWING A PLAN

Your allowance is money to spend as you wish. Don't get in the habit of overspending in other places and using an allowance to make up the excess spending. Guard your freedom to spend some money as you alone intend, to preserve your sanity.

Always review the family's plan before going shopping as a reminder of goals. This helps avoid impulse buying and other vices that steer you off course.

Remember, a budget is a plan, nothing more. It is not the criminal code. Don't use it as law to convict or punish family members. If you spend more than a planned amount, look for ways to make it up.

Don't fight poor cost estimates. If you consistently overspend a planned amount, revise your plan to set a more realistic amount. Make small spending corrections as needed. If you splurge one month and hope to get back on the track of family wants, go on a money diet and tighten up spending next month.

Don't make a habit of changing your mind about family wishes. If you want to purchase an item that is not on your plan, allow a cooling off period before buying it. And adjust your plan to see what goals will be given up to acquire it. If you are still interested after all of this, and you can persuade the family council, go ahead and buy. You deserve it.

Tape a list of family goals to the inside cover of your checkbook or wallet. This keeps them in front of you while spending. And make it a habit of writing down a description of each purchase.

Don't plan to make up overspending for some items by saving money on medical outlays. The minute a savings in medical expense appears likely and you count on it, the odds triple that someone in the family will break a leg, a tooth, or a neck, requiring medical attention.

Table 20

TRAPS TO AVOID

Con Artists	"Mom, I've already spent my allowance. Will you buy this record album with your money? I'll pay you back next month."
Logic	"It's not the kind of purchase we can wait on. We need shrubbery and trees now. They take forty-eight years to grow. We can't wait or we'll be dead first."
Timing	"Can you fix it where I can buy this coat on next month's budget now?"
Underground Purchasing	"Does this lay-away slip have anything to do with eating hamburger every night this week?"
Shifting The Wants	"I just had a flat tire coming home from the poker game. I had to buy a new one at George's store. It's a good thing he was playing tonight."
Rigid Planning	"Spot just bit a car and he's going to need stitches. It's too bad he overspent his allowance."

7

A Family Money Picture

How much are you worth? Answer this riddle and your family's money picture can be put on the screen in living color. If, by some chance, you don't know your worth, you can adjust the dials, turn the antenna, or kick the set, and for all of this effort, not even a glimpse of the picture will appear, let alone a panoramic view. But then, some people hate to admit defeat. My cousin, Wilber, once roasted his television over an open fire because it quit during a Super Bowl telecast. His set never worked again, but Wilber swears it was the best thing he ever did. Even so, he missed the rest of the game, and you will, too, by trying this or similar measures with your money picture. To see it, you must first solve the riddle of your worth.

As expected, this solution requires a little effort and ingenuity. First, you need to know about assets and liabilities. These terms don't refer directly to family members, although you are entitled to your own suspicions. For a money picture, think of assets and liabilities with a fence between them. On one side of the fence is everything your family owns—assets. On the other side are the things that you owe— liabilities. And it's not difficult to figure out the side of the fence on which most things belong.

True, this information and a quarter can do wonders in a phone booth. And true again, most people know these things, or at least the difference between assets and liabilities. But what many of them don't know is how these components work together to present a picture of

83

ASSETS

DEBTS

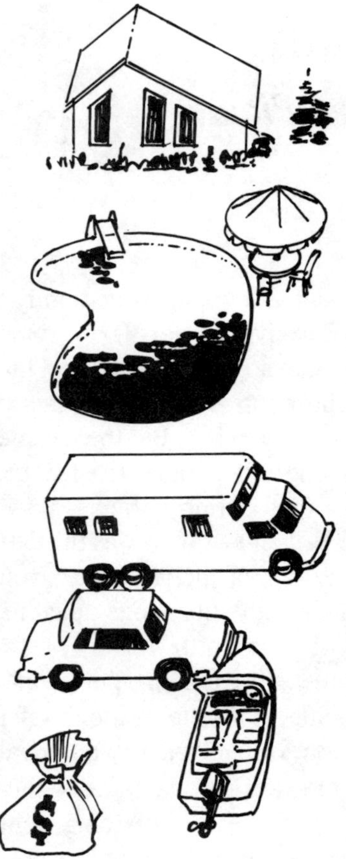

NET WORTH

TOTAL $$

TOTAL $$

family finances. If they did, loan officers across the country wouldn't receive balance sheets that are not balanced. And people wouldn't part with their financial information so nonchalantly if they knew its potential to help them win the money game.

Knowing how each component of a money picture works is different from knowing, for example, that assets are a major component. After all, the plug on a television that fits in the wall socket is a component of your set. Does knowing this tell you how a television works? Does it explain why, if the black wire is crossed with the red one inside the TV, your hair will stand on end? No. To understand these things, you must know how each component works. In the same way, knowing how the parts of a money picture work insures that you don't get your wires crossed later. So sit back and take a refresher course to see how your picture works. Later on, you can watch some dazzling displays.

Adding Up Assets

Anything that a family can claim as rightful and legal owner belongs on the asset side of the fence. The difficulty is figuring out the value of the things that are owned. For instance, a home may be one of your biggest assets in terms of value. But it is not how much it cost or how much money is remaining on the mortgage that counts here. What counts is the price your home would bring if sold today. To find this amount, look at prices that similar houses are selling for in your neighborhood. Or, talk to lenders who finance homes. They can provide an idea of the value of any castle on the block, including your own.

Of course, some assets, like cash in bank accounts, are valued at their face amount. Fifty cents in the bank is worth fifty cents. Make the amount a million dollars in savings and you have a million dollars—plus a lot of friends; but you can't count them. Other assets, like the car, the furniture, or Aunt Sally's antique tea kettle require an estimate of value to put them on your picture. To make these estimates, you can consult dealers, price guides, or the classified ad section of the newspaper. Or, if all else fails, make an educated guess on how much money these kind of assets would bring if sold. Just make certain your estimates are realistic. And don't forget to put a value on the stocks or bonds that are owned, or even life insurance policies. Again, the key to valuing these or any other assets is the price they would bring if sold. The value of life insurance policies is the amount that would be received if they were surrendered to the company. If they don't have any cash value, your policies are worthless as long as you are alive. True, they may be worth a fortune once you are dead, but in this case, you will be the last to know.

When a value has been placed on the things that are owned, add the numbers for a grand total of assets.

Adding Up Debts

On the liability side of the fence are debts, including everything from a mortgage right on down to the light bill that hasn't been paid yet. Balances due on charge accounts, bank loans outstanding, and any other debts belong here. Sure, it's easy to think of a hundred other things more pleasant than calling to mind your debts. But if you intend to find your worth, don't treat this task lightly and forget some of them. Creditors have long memories. It is doubtful that the people you owe will forget about the money, so include all debts on this side of the fence. Even Uncle Sam, who seldom forgets a face, expects to receive any taxes that might be due over and above the amounts withheld in a paycheck. Include them.

When you have completed a listing of this group, add the numbers on this side of the fence for a total of debts.

How Much Are You Worth?

In official circles at least, your worth is known as your "net worth." It is *net* because it is the difference between total assets and total liabilities. To solve the riddle, subtract the total of the amount you owe the rest of the world from the total of what your family owns. Or, if you are big on formulas, assets minus liabilities equals net worth.*

---

*   With more debts than assets, you are subtracting a larger number from a smaller one. This is still as much fun as it was back in the fourth grade. In short, if debts exceed assets, you have a negative net worth. This doesn't mean you are worthless, but it does mean that your family owes more money than the value of assets. Take steps to improve net worth if it is negative. Try reducing debt or increasing assets without adding additional debt. It won't be easy, but a negative net worth can be turned into a positive number. Most people have a positive net worth and the sooner you move yours into this status, the better.

Focusing The Picture

So where is your money picture? Yes, well, you probably turned your antenna. But if you are still having trouble seeing it, the problem may be with you rather than the picture. You simply need to know how to look at it. Maybe this will help: start with the picket fence that separates assets and liabilities. All those wonderful things that your family owns, including the kitchen sink, are on the asset side. Take a closer look. Your car is there, although from the looks of it, you ought to wash it. The house, the lawn, the greenbacks in your bank account—these assets are in the picture, or they should be. As rightful and legal owner of all these things, take an inventory to make sure everything in your vast holdings has been included. While making this inventory, notice how many assets could quickly be converted to cash in case you need to get out of town in a hurry. This information can be helpful later.

On the other side of the fence, the liability side, are your debts. All the businesses, government agencies, and people who are your creditors are in this happy group. Do you recognize them? You should, since they seem to know you. Anyone left out is probably expecting more than an honorable mention, so check your list again. And don't think of this group too harshly. After all, they loaned the money in one way or another so your family could buy some of those assets on the other side of the fence. Without their generous help, your asset list would be smaller.

Strange as it may seem, net worth belongs on the same side of the fence as debts. Obviously, net worth and debts are not the same thing; which means they must have something in common. Strange, but true; they do. Debts and net worth are the money sources that finance all your wonderful assets. This means some assets are financed by loans and others by net worth. Think of it this way: your house, which you probably didn't buy with the loose change in your pocket, is financed partly by the mortgage—a debt—and partly by equity, or worth. And your house can thank its lucky stars that the guys on the other side of the fence—your mortgage and worth—came up with the money. Otherwise, your family wouldn't be living there. When looking at your picture, remember that everything on this side of the fence is the money source for assets on the other side.

Are You Getting Ahead?

Once your money picture is in focus, you can do a lot of things with it. For one, it's possible to measure how much net worth is growing from one year to the next. Since assets and liabilities change almost daily, a money picture shows the position of family finances on a particular date. To compare your worth from one year to the next, simply build a new picture next year. Then compare the difference in net worth on both occasions. By checking the amount now and next year or even six months from now, you can measure how much your worth is growing. If it isn't growing, your family is not getting ahead.

Naturally, it helps to know what increases net worth. Earning a paycheck increases it. Conversely, spending all your earnings on food decreases net worth, though it may increase your waistline. In short, if you eat up all your income, you won't be getting ahead. All things considered, there are two ways to spend money. You can either use it to buy things that grow in value or are supposed to grow, such as stocks, bonds, real estate, or similar things; or it can be used to buy things that depreciate in value, such as cars, stereos, and entertainment, to name a few. In practice, people spend their money in both of these ways. But the more money that can be spent on investments that grow in value, the more net worth increases. If you spend money this way, if the things actually bought grow in value, and if they grow fast, other people may say that you are worth a fortune. And it could be true. However, there isn't much to gain in becoming worth a fortune by starving in the process. The best approach is to find a reasonable balance between the things that grow in value and the things that don't, but that are needed anyway to make life a more pleasurable experience. With this approach, you can steadily increase net worth from one year to the next, while having fun along the way.

Testing Ideas

A money picture can also show a preview of how new opportunities will affect net worth. Say, for instance, you are thinking of selling your home. Unless you plan on taking chickens and goats in trade, some money should be received at the closing. And the lender who holds the mortgage is going to be there alert as a squirrel when you get the cash. So the first thing to do is to pay off the mortgage. This entitles you to throw this debt off the liability side of your picture and break out the champagne. Since you plan to make a bundle of money on this deal, put the cash left over on the asset side of the fence under cash assets. Needless to say, you will wave goodbye to your home and remove it from the list of assets. And now, for the moment of truth, add up assets and liabilities again to see how much your net worth has changed from all this wheeling and dealing. Simply subtract the new total of liabilities from the asset total to find your new worth. Your family is now living out in the street, but at least everyone will be impressed with your bank account, if not your accommodations. But more importantly, you can see how the idea of selling the house will affect your family's picture. Best of all, you can see it before actually doing it.

Adjusting The Picture

Other money decisions can be tested in the same way as long as you understand how the components work. To keep a picture in focus, the totals on both sides of the fence must be equal—always. Regardless of what adjustments are made, total assets must always equal total debts and worth. Now, if this little detail is forgotten, you might as well cross the red wire with the black one inside your television set. The outcome is the same. Your money picture goes up in a puff of smoke and the lights go out. Which is why I repeat: never fool around with the wires inside a television set and keep the totals on both sides of the fence equal on your picture.

Can you still test money decisions by changing the numbers around on a money picture? Absolutely. But when all of the adjustments and changes are made, make sure the totals on both sides of the fence are equal. For example, let's say that you found a million tax-free dollars in the street and put them in a bank account. This does wonders for your cash asset, not to mention the treatment you will receive the next time in the bank. Moreover, the total of all your assets is increased by a million dollars. On the other side of the fence, you obviously didn't increase debts; which means your net worth has changed. As luck would have it, the million dollars found in the street just increased net worth by the same amount. Why else would bankers fall all over themselves on your entrance? Your money picture is still in focus because both sides of the fence are equal.

Some money decisions can affect only one side of the fence. Say for instance, the boss's son, Junior, who once sold encyclopedias and has managed to complicate your life ever since, is now selling stocks. And heaven forbid that you should not buy a good, safe stock from Junior. So while the boss looks on approvingly, Junior sells you this great little stock that promises riches in hardly no time at all. Of course, you, former buyer of encyclopedias, are wiser now. You buy a few shares of stock for five hundred dollars tops. Everyone is happy. Junior made his sale and the boss is smiling. So what happened to your money picture? To find out, subtract five hundred from cash assets and pay Junior. Then add the shares of stock to a new asset called investment. Since you subtracted five hundred from one asset and added it to another, the total on this side of the fence remains unchanged. Your picture is still in balance because nothing was adjusted on the other side. Of course, when buying stock from Junior, you should celebrate the same day. Tomorrow, the stock will likely be trading for a fraction of the price you paid. And tomorrow, you can remind yourself not to buy anything from Junior ever again.

Seeing Trouble Ahead

The monies used to leave town in a hurry are the same dollars needed in a cash squeeze. Few of us need lessons on getting into a cash squeeze. Avoiding one is something we could all use. Add up your family's assets that are cash or easily converted to cash. These include stocks, bonds, savings certificates, and similar items. Next, add a total of payments on debts that will come due in the coming year. To check your susceptibility to the cash squeeze, divide the total of cash or near cash assets by the total of debt payments due in the coming year. The result is called a quick ratio, which probably comes from the folks who were getting out of town in a hurry. With ten thousand dollars in assets that are cash or close to it and five thousand in debts payable next year, your ratio is two to one. This means that for every dollar of debt that is coming due next year, you have two dollars in cash or similar assets to pay for it. That's not a bad position to be in. If your ratio is one to one, you have one dollar of debt for every dollar of cash or near–cash assets. In this situation, you don't need more debt—or at least additional debt that requires any payments in the coming year. With a ratio of one-half to one, more debt is coming due than you have funds to pay it. Welcome to the cash squeeze. To get out of this bind, you can sell other assets, converting them to cash, or refinance part of your debt so that less of it comes due in the year ahead. Unless you discover a pot of gold at the end of the rainbow, make plans to avoid the cash squeeze. Naturally, it's nice to know when trouble is ahead to have the time to do something about it.

So Who Owns Whom?

Since debts and net worth are the money sources for assets, certain creditors may have claims on your family's possessions. The question is, who has a greater claim—you or the creditors? It's easy enough to find out. Compare the total of debts with your worth. With more debt than worth, creditors have more claims on your assets than you do. If net worth is more than debts, you are the majority stockholder of family assets—which is as it should be. Everyone has his own idea of how much debt is the right amount. Some people loath the idea of being in debt. Other's swear by it, saying debt is the best way to get ahead financially. Probably the best approach is somewhere in between these two philosophies. But if you prefer holding the majority interest in family assets, don't feel alone. Nothing quite replaces the old-fashioned notion that what is yours is yours.

Tapping Picture Power

If your money picture could attract dollars, would you use it? Whenever I ask people this question, they say yes. Well okay, maybe a few of them answer more emphatically and say, hail yes; but mostly these are religious folks. Even so, what they soon discover is that a money picture can help acquire a loan when they need one. Since credit is an important part of almost everyone's finances these days, you might be interested in knowing how banks and others make the decision to lend money.

Many of them use a scoring system. (And all this time you thought it was your charm.) Sad to say, it often comes down to points. A good credit history may net forty points. Owning a home might add another twenty points. A steady job, good income, and you've been there forever—take maybe thirty points. At the end of this process, they total the score. A solid citizen with a good credit history, good income, and few installment debts might earn a hundred points. Another person who has held ten different jobs in the last nine days might score a two—one for breathing and the other for having the guts to ask for the loan. While every scoring system is different, each one has a score, below which aspiring applicants are politely turned down. Now, if the Sleepy Hollow Bank where you live doesn't use a scoring system, don't worry about it. Not all lenders do. But even at Sleepy Hollow, they make loan decisions based on the same principles. These principles are known as the three Cs of credit: character, capacity, and collateral. Character refers to you. Capacity means your ability to repay, and collateral is what is sometimes put up to make sure you do. Scoring system or not, that's how lenders decide.

A money picture can't do all the work to garner a loan. A good credit history is important. Making payments to other creditors on time impresses lenders. Conversely, if you consistently pay late, they figure that their loan is going to receive the same treatment. So even if you pay promptly most of the time, check your credit history by asking to see your file at a local credit bureau. You may pay a small fee, but it is worth the money. If a disgruntled store has saddled your history with a credit blight, it can be explained or challenged and in some cases, removed. Any inaccurate information that detracts from your good credit standing should be corrected, even if it means going back to the store and asking for the correction. If the store's credit department balks, remind them about all your relatives who used to shop there.

Nothing catches a lender's eye more than income. He wants to know how much it is, how stable it is, and what portion of your income goes to pay on other debts. The reason for this curiosity is because income says alot about your capacity to repay. A forty-thousand-dollar-a-year income is not going to justify a forty-thousand-dollar loan at the bank, because they figure the money won't be paid back in this century. Banks are short-term lenders, meaning a year or two suits them just fine, and six months is even better. Centuries are definitely out. Other lenders will spring for long–term loans, but they, too, will measure income against the amount of the loan. A money picture can help, but it won't make up for insufficient income.

So how do you spruce up your picture to attract a loan? Simply mold it in the right shape. If debt payments, not counting your mortgage, already consume twenty-five percent of your income, most lenders are reluctant to lend additional dollars. Knowing this, you can start managing your finances to get debts to fit this guideline. Just leave some additional room below the limit. If making the loan means pushing your installment debts past the twenty-five percent mark, few lenders will jump at the chance.

Similarly, if debts are excessive compared to assets, this tells lenders that your assets are probably mortgaged to the hilt. To improve your picture, reduce debts to a smaller proportion of your assets. Lenders look at assets for collateral. When a loan is not justified on your signature alone, pledging an asset as collateral can sometimes swing the decision in your favor. For these occasions, it's wise to keep some possessions free and clear of creditor claims. Just don't volunteer collateral unless it is absolutely necessary. And when it is, don't offer to pledge your lawn mower. Lenders prefer more substantial assets as collateral. Your gold bullion is fine with them.

But tapping the power of your money picture is more than simply molding it into the right shape. To get the most out of it, show a loan officer that you understand your finances. You'd be amazed at the number of people who have no idea how their picture works. Don't join this crowd. Don't hand over financial information piece by piece when applying for a loan. Know what your credit report says before the loan officer knows. Allow him to see your plans, how you expect to repay the loan, and what the effects will be on your money picture. And let him know the downside risks and that you've taken them into account. If you win his confidence, he can make the difference when a scoring system says the loan is marginal. He wants to help, but he won't risk his job to do it. The best approach is to be honest, calm a loan officer's fear of making a bad loan, and strive for a long-term business relationship with him. If he advises against a loan, consider his advice. The credit tests work to your advantage, too. The loan you don't need is the one that cannot be repaid.

A family money picture in the right shape has power to attract money. By keeping debts in line with income and demonstrating an ability to manage your finances, you can tap this power. Credit is no small matter for most of us. Over our lifetimes, we borrow money extensively, in both good and bad economic times. Credit provides flexibility to take advantage of opportunity in our lives. By using picture power, we can make sure that the money is there when it's needed.

Super Planning To Mesh Family Goals

How would you like your money picture to appear in the future? Some people call this dreaming. Financial people call it pro forma analysis, which is similar to saying that your picture will be in a certain position on a future date, no matter what freezes over. Here's how it might work.

For instance, let's say your family wishes to have one hundred thousand in cash (small bills, please) at age sixty-five. Say also, that another desire is to have a paid-up mortgage on the house. And for good measure, let's throw in a supplemental investment income of 12 thousand per year. Now, how can you build this picture? Easy. Build it by writing each goal on your future money picture, as if you'd already obtained it. Under cash assets, write one hundred thousand dollars, just as you said. Your home should be on the asset side at some projected value in the future, considering inflation. On the liability side of the fence, not a trace of a mortgage should show up, since part of the plan was to pay it off.

An investment belongs on the asset side that will yield the desired monthly income. Here's where some arithmetic is required. For example, if you believe a 12 percent return can be earned on your investments, you'd need investment assets of one hundred thousand dollars to provide the supplemental income desired ($12,000 divided by 12 percent). Depending upon your interests, this investment might represent the cost of rental properties, bonds, or a portfolio of stocks. Once all goals are on the picture, add up the numbers to find your projected net worth in the rosy future. If everything comes true, this is where you will be.

The next question is how to get there. To find the steps needed, simply subtract your present money picture from the one desired for the future. This shows what changes must be made in the meantime. With ten thousand in cash now, another ninety thousand is needed to reach your target. How much time is remaining to obtain this amount? If an IRA won't provide the money, what other activities might provide it? If thirty thousand dollars is the balance left on the house mortgage, you'll need a payment schedule that retires this debt by the time age sixty–five rolls around. If current monthly payments won't do it, find a schedule that will meet your goal. With no investment income now, you need to make some investments, maybe buying an annuity that will pay the desired income after age sixty-five or picking up rental properties to assure this income. This kind of powerful analysis—building a desired money picture for the future and comparing it with your present picture—can put a lot of goals in perspective, at the same time showing the amounts needed to reach them. It's a great way to mesh different family goals together in one package to see how they fit and what is required to achieve them.

Common Sense

When all is said and done, the important thing is to view your money picture with that not-so-common commodity, common sense. If you have very little money in cash assets, it's wise to increase cash or similar assets before buying things that are not so easily converted to cash. If debts are consuming too much of your income, you don't need additional debt right now. If you have assets that are no longer needed or desired, sell them. If the price they bring is less than their value, your net worth will decrease. If more money is received than their value by selling them, you will increase net worth. These common sense guidelines work.

But one of the best uses of a picture is for planning. Whether merely testing a new idea to see the effect on net worth or meshing long-term family goals, planning provides a view of the options on your financial horizon. It's a view that many families seldom see.

Table 21

YOUR FAMILY MONEY PICTURE

ASSETS		DEBTS AND WORTH	
"Quick" Assets:		Debts Due In The Coming Year:	
Cash, checking, savings accounts	$ _______	Monthly bills due	$ _______
Saving certificates	$ _______	Credit card balances	$ _______
Money market funds	$ _______	Portion of installment loans due	$ _______
Cash value of life insurance policies	$ _______	Portion of mortgage balance due	$ _______
Other quick assets	$ _______	Personal loans	$ _______
	$ _______	Unpaid income taxes	$ _______
	$ _______	Other taxes	$ _______
	$ _______	Amounts due to brokers	$ _______
Total "Quick" Assets	$ _______	Total Debts Due In The Next Twelve Months	$ _______
Investment Assets:		Long-Term Debts:	
Notes owed to you	$ _______	Portion of installment loans due after next year	$ _______
Stocks	$ _______		
Bonds	$ _______	Mortgage balance due after the coming year	$ _______
Real estate held for investment	$ _______	Money you owe relatives	$ _______
Other investments	$ _______	Any other long-term debts	$ _______
Retirement funds			
Total Investment Assets	$ _______	Total Long-Term Debts	$ _______
Personal Assets:			
Your home	$ _______		
Furnishings	$ _______		
Automobiles	$ _______		
Recreational vehicles	$ _______	Your Family's Net Worth	$ _______
Other personal assets	$ _______		
Total Personal Assets	$ _______		
GRAND TOTAL OF YOUR WONDERFUL ASSETS	$ _______	**GRAND TOTAL OF DEBTS AND YOUR FAMILY'S NET WORTH**	$ _______

8

Protection

You need protection. If you don't believe it, accidently ram into your neighbor's car while backing out of the driveway. Then watch what happens. With any luck at all, your neighbor will bolt out of his house like a wounded bear before you can say shucks or the name of your insurance company. This just goes to show that people regard their assets as prized possessions, worth twice as much as before, if you should damage one of them.

"Aw C'mon, Harry," you say. "It's only a rear fender. How much could a replacement possibly cost?"

"The car was an antique," Harry whines. "Besides, what about the whip-lash?"

"For heaven's sake, Harry, you weren't even in the car."

"Yea, but when I heard the sound of metal being crushed, I turned my head so fast to see that I injured my neck."

Don't laugh. Harry can show up in court wearing a neck brace, whimpering slightly, and a sympathetic jury might award him enough money to buy a hundred new cars, plus the fender you owe him. It happens. And that's precisely why you need protection.

Life is full of hazards that can ruin your day, not to mention short-circuiting your money picture. These calamities can be dealt with in several ways. For starters, don't walk under ladders and avoid black cats. If these two don't cause your demise, a tornado or hurricane could be the next on the agenda. Unless protection is provided in the form of insurance, you'd better take a snapshot of your money picture. If a disaster comes along, it may be the only memento that remains.

Life Insurance

People get the wrong idea about insurance. Not that they start out this way, mind you. They only get cynical about insurance after paying the premiums for a while and collecting nothing on their policy. Say, for instance, you buy an insurance policy on your life. But you don't die right away. Instead, you linger on for maybe another fifty years. Now at some point during this time, usually when a premium due date rolls around, you will begin to think that money is being paid out for no worthwhile benefit. Send in your premium anyway. You didn't buy life insurance to collect on it. You bought it to protect your family in case you die and leave them behind. The last thing they will need then is to be forced to sell the house or other assets because you didn't provide for their future.

And still the odd notions about life insurance persist. Here are a few of them:

"If I die, Doris, you and the kids are going to be rich."

True, if Doris's husband dies, they could be rich, depending upon the amount of insurance on his life and the estate taxes. But why advertise that you are worth more dead than alive? Yet husbands do.

And what about Doris? She has a good job and manages to be a homemaker, too. If something happens to her, the family's second income won't be coming in anymore. A housekeeper to replace her services in the home won't be cheap either. She should have as much insurance as her advertising husband. Does she have it? Probably not. People still think that women need less insurance than men.

Life insurance on children doesn't make a lot of sense, but people continue to buy it in large amounts. True, the kids should have some insurance, but probably no more than is necessary to cover final expenses.

The amount of life insurance needed depends on what the proceeds are intended to accomplish. Once you know the purpose, it's not difficult to figure how much insurance is needed. Yet people think nothing of allowing an agent to make this judgment for them. Other vendors would love the same opportunity with their wares, but no such luck. People will buy everything else on their own decision. It's enough to make you feel sorry for the insurance folks.

Health Protection

If people who buy life insurance seem cynical, ask a few of them who have health insurance.

My friend, Jim, has a health insurance policy that covers everyone in his family.

"It's a great policy," he told me half-jokingly. "We are never in the dark about what it covers. If anyone of us gets sick, whatever the malady, this policy pays nothing."

"Well, that eliminates the guesswork," I said.

"Yes, but you should see the premiums," he replied.

"How much do you pay for it?" I asked.

"One hundred sixty dollars a month."

"And it covers nothing?"

"Well, a few things are covered," he admitted, "but I have yet to collect on one of them."

"Maybe you ought to get the kind of policy that Joe has," I said. "His policy pays if he gets chapped lips."

Of course, Joe's policy is expensive, the kind that an Arab oil minister might afford. But Joe's company pays for his family's health insurance, which is why Joe, who is neither an Arab nor an oil minister, can afford it. The rest of the folks who are not employed by a behemoth corporation like Joe don't get this policy. Instead, they get chapped lips or some other marvelous condition that is not covered under their policies.

But people don't become cynical for nothing. Somewhere in this maze of confusion called the health insurance business is someone who understands it. Whoever he is, he is not your agent. Your agent understands his company's products, which is different from knowing why premiums increase geometrically. Even so, anyone who can explain a health insurance policy well enough to convince people to pay money for it is unusually bright, gifted, and ought not to be thrown out of the house; at least not until you learn what his policy covers and how it compares in cost with the competition.

When it comes to health insurance, it pays to shop. It also pays to know what a policy covers. You can be fluent in five languages and still be confused by the medical terms and insurance jargon in these policies. Even agents, who are trained to know the difference between a wart and a brain tumor, can have trouble explaining exactly what is included. This may not seem important, unless you consider that the cost of a hospital stay can wipe out assets and net worth almost overnight.

People don't plan on paying five hundred dollars for x-rays. No one plans these things. Who would guess that hospital lab work could amount to a month's wages. After all, the hospital ought to pay you for a urine sample. But serious medical problems don't always strike someone else. Sometimes they can hit your family. If and when they do, you will need health insurance protection. Without it, you play for high stakes. Granted, you may save the cost of premiums. But if a family member does become seriously ill, your risk savings and other assets accumulated over the years to pay the medical bills. It is surprising how many people work hard to build up their nest egg and give no thought to protecting it.

More often than not, group health insurance plans offer the best coverage for the money. If you don't belong to a group, join one. A friend of mine changes his health insurance regularly and thinks nothing of it. At the first mention of a rate increase, he finds some new association to join that has an excellent group health policy at lower rates. Try his technique and you may occasionally find yourself in odd company. But then, you and the rest of the "Bull Shooters of America" can snicker at the rates the rest of us are paying for health insurance.

Of course, if you wouldn't be caught dead with a group like the Bull Shooters, buy your own policy. Individual policies are often more expensive than coverage through a group, but you can still lower the cost of premiums. Accepting higher deductibles can result in a lower rate. Or, buy a policy that covers only major illness and cover the cost of minor medical problems yourself. Never mind that the policy doesn't cover bandaids. As long as protection is the goal, you should guard against the really serious injury or illness that can play havoc with the family finances. Just be certain to know what risks are being covered out of your own pocket. Paying for office visits is one thing. But picking up the tab for major surgery is something better left to insurance companies.

Whatever you do, don't buy a policy that protects against one illness, like cancer. These policies prey on people's fear of a particular disease, and they are almost never worth the price. Buying health protection this way is like playing Russian Roulette with your money picture. Invariably, you won't get sick with whatever is covered in these policies. Any health policy should provide a broad range of coverage. Usually, this is accomplished through major-medical coverage, which helps pay for virtually any type of medical care. On second thought, if you already have a policy with this sweeping coverage, buy the one that protects against a single illness. This improves the odds that you won't come down with the disease. But make this the limit of your gambling on health protection. Remember, medical science can work wonders to keep your family healthy. It's up to you to make sure your money picture doesn't become ill in the process.

Protecting The Castle

Lots of things can happen to a home. A tornado can lift the roof from your house and deposit it in the next county. It can be ransacked by burglars, leaving little more than bare walls and an empty cupboard. Or, a produce truck can make a delivery in your living room. This may not send you scurrying to buy homeowner's insurance, but it ought to scare the socks off the lender who holds the mortgage. Lenders are jittery about these things. Your home is one of your biggest assets. If it should burn down, you are exposed to serious loss. This concerns a lender, almost as much as what the price of charred wood or used brick might bring on a foreclosure sale. Suffice to say, you probably have homeowner's insurance, if you own a home.

So why am I telling you about homeowner's insurance, if lenders insist on it anyway? Because some lenders have trouble reading any fine print that is not their own. And insurance policies have fine print, the kind that says who is going to pay if a disaster comes along. A basic homeowner's policy will cover a loss from fire. But it may not cover damage from a tree that falls through the roof or water damage from broken pipes. There are different levels of protection from which to choose. And the time to choose is before a loss, not afterward. If in doubt, buy an all-risk policy. It will cover everything except earthquakes, mud slides, acts of war, floods, nuclear hazards and maybe a few other things, depending upon the insurer. This may not sound like an all-risk policy, but then, you ought to see the basic policy. Meanwhile, the all-risk protection is the best available.

Once you know the risks that are covered, it's simply a question of how much money the insurer will pay in the event of a loss. Say, for example, your home floats away as a result of broken water pipes that your cousin Mort fixed last Tuesday. Your first instinct will be to load up a shotgun and find Mort. Don't do it. Call the insurance company first. If damage from broken pipes is included in the policy, and the coverage limits have been kept up to date with escalating housing values, the company should pay to rebuild your home. On the other hand, if the policy provides all the money needed to rebuild at 1948 prices, you'd better find Mort. The insurance money might be barely enough to construct a deluxe outhouse, let alone replace your home. It pays to check the coverage limits of a policy. Some policies offer automatic adjustments to these limits to keep them in line with inflation. Or a policy can be bought to replace a home no matter what the costs, if you agree to insure for what the company thinks the home is worth. Either way, don't depend on the mortgage-holder to select the proper coverage. Make certain the protection is adequate in case of a loss. Otherwise, homeowner's insurance won't do the job it was intended to do.

Can the cost of protecting your castle be reduced? Well, yes and no. The easiest way to reduce premiums is to accept higher deductibles. The catch is that if there is a loss, you pay out more money. Insurance companies do give discounts for security alarms and smoke detectors. Unfortunately, these items often cost more than what can be saved on premiums. Of course, if a security system was planned anyway, take the discount. And next time your family has a change of address, select a home closer to a fire hydrant. This can acquaint you with the dogs in the neighborhood and lower insurance premiums at the same time.

How Much Protection Do You Need?

A good time to check protection is after your money picture is focused. This is when you can play the What-If Game. Just ask the right questions. What happens if your car is wrecked? A rear clip, meaning everything replaced from the back seats to the rear bumper might cost five thousand dollars for your automobile. Without insurance, you will take the money out of your cash assets to pay for the repairs. With collision coverage, you will pay the deductible amount. With choices like this one, it's easy to see that protection is worthwhile. What happens if your jewelry is stolen? Or, what happens if the jury awards Harry damages for his neck because you cratered his antique car? Do you have enough liability protection or will Harry's lawyers extract the money from you? Liability limits can easily be increased on insurance policies and the cost is usually minimal. The catch is that you have to ask for the higher protection.

To play the *What-If* Game, drag out your insurance policies and read them. Granted, they won't read like a novel, but checking protection is worth the effort. Besides, you are not reading for entertainment. The idea is to learn what is covered and what is not. If you want to be entertained, try reading these policies after a loss. Then you can be thrilled at the suspense of every word, wondering whether or not you have the protection.

Don't be shy with your what-if questions. Just come right out and ask them. What happens if you gag on the roast beef tomorrow and choke to death? Yes, sure, the funeral home will give you a nice send-off. But afterwards, what happens to your family? How much money will they have to live on? To find out, add up all of the policies that are payable upon your demise. How many years will this amount last if it is spent to cover expenses each year? Use your family's present spending as a guide.* If your family needs thirty thousand dollars per year for expenses now, and you have a hundred and fifty thousand dollars worth of life insurance, it should last at least five years, and perhaps longer if the money is invested to earn interest or dividends. It comes down to weighing how much money will be needed each year, how many years you want this amount to be received, and how much the policies provide. If more coverage is desired, weigh the amount against what you can afford. Then make the best choice.

Checking other types of insurance works the same way. Ask what-if questions and find the answers in the policies. If burglars take the silverware, how much will your homeowner's policy pay? If you rent an apartment, how much money will renter's insurance pay for personal possessions lost in a fire? The common mistake is not asking enough questions. Against better judgment, I told my neighbor about the what-if questions one evening. A few days later, his wife, thrilled

---

* Some advisors say your family can get by on two-thirds of your present income if you are gone. Obviously, these people don't know your family.

at the idea, reported that they asked what would happen if the collision coverage was dropped on their second car? As it turned out, they saved sixty dollars by dropping this coverage on a car that wasn't worth much when it was new, let alone twenty years later. And this, she proudly reported, was the vast sum total of all their questions. Why at this rate, she thought they could save untold sums of money by just asking one question a week. They had better save untold sums, because they will need them, considering all the holes in their protection. The what-if questions are designed to check coverages for gaps in protection, not to save money. If they occasionally result in savings, fine. But that's not the purpose for asking.

Checking Exclusions

To find out if your protection has gaps in coverage, check the exclusions in your policies. You won't have any trouble finding the exclusions. They are usually written in plain English. It's the coverage portions of policies that are sometimes baffling. Even so, exclusions tell what risks you are covering, which makes them worth knowing. If a homeowner's policy doesn't cover floods and you live in an area likely to be flooded, you may wish to seek flood insurance from the federal government at a nominal price. If health insurance doesn't include disability pay in case of extended illness, a separate policy can be bought to add this coverage. But don't assume that because a risk isn't covered in one policy that it won't be covered in another. Check all policies. Any risks not covered can be shifted to an insurer if the coverage is available.

As a practical matter, you can't protect against every possible hazard. But you can guard against most of them or at least soften their effects. Remember, insurance is not purchased to collect on it. It is bought for protection and the peace of mind that comes from having it. No one forces you to buy the protection. But by choosing not to buy, you take all the risks. In this case, the costs can be enormous if you lose.

Table 22

SUGGESTIONS FOR PROTECTION

The surest way to lower premiums on any insurance is to accept higher deductible amounts. The wisdom of doing so depends on the type of insurance and your ability to pay the deductible in case of a loss.

Seek advice. An independent agent is a good source. He knows how to shop insurance, and he is usually abreast of changes in the insurance business that can affect you. But don't become a basket-case once in the door. If you buy his products, insist on value.

Buy renewable term life insurance. You get what you pay for—insurance. Whole life policies are a combination of savings and insurance. If you buy one of these, make certain the return on the savings portion is as good or better than is available elsewhere.

Aim for enough life insurance on a breadwinner to replace at least five years worth of his or her income. Consider additional coverage to pay off a mortgage or to fund educational needs, depending your own circumstances.

Health insurance should have major-medical coverage in the event of catastrophic illness. Don't insure for things that you can pay yourself.

Homeowner's insurance covers a home and its contents, which often amount to a majority of your assets. Buy an all-risk policy from a reputable company.

Take an inventory of your personal property, preferably one that includes photographs of that property. This avoids a lot of quibbling if there is a claim.

Insure for higher liability protection. Basic coverage limits under most policies are generally too low for today's legal environment.

9

Winning The Money Game

Your late Aunt Hilda, bless her soul, may have told you that winning isn't everything, it is how the game is played that counts. Of course, Aunt Hilda is long-since gone; she probably wrote you out of her will anyway and gave that passing advice to test your mettle. If it wasn't Aunt Hilda, then another relative may have told a similar story about winning.

As it turns out, Aunt Hilda's advice was half-right. How you play the game does count. But it is no substitute for winning. Just ask the younger kids who play sports. The six- and seven–year–olds on the soccer team that I coach can tell you about sportsmanship. They also know the difference between winning and losing. I've heard well-meaning parents comfort their children after a distressing game loss by telling them, "We can't all be winners." Fortunately, the kids know better, they don't believe a word of it, and play the next game to win. Winning is everything when it comes to getting family wants. Granted, you may have a setback or two, but since this is the money game, take a lesson from the children and play it to win.

In America, you live in a country where all of us have the opportunity to be winners, if we try. You don't need to put someone else in the poor house to win the money game. Nor is it necessary to take unfair advantage of others to win. On the contrary, by pursuing your family goals vigorously, you will be opening up opportunities for others to obtain the things they want as well. How is this possible?

It is possible because we have the freedom in this country to choose our own wants. And we don't all seek the same things in life. When pursuing your own choices, you create opportunities for others to supply them. By paying for them, you provide the income for others to buy their favorite choices as well. When you sit back and figure that you can't win, that others are more fortunate than you are, and that you can't beat the system, that is when you will lose. Unfortunately, the rest of us will lose right along with you.

But it is not necessary to worry about other people's wants. Just concentrate on your family's favorite choices. By taking care of these, you will be doing a good turn for the rest of us. And since the rest of us stand to benefit from your success, we think you should look at all the ways to win and lose the money game. Knowing them, you can do all the right things to win.

Get-Rich-Quick Schemes

As it turns out, few people sign up for the nose–dive trip by not paying attention to their finances. While they may not pay as much attention as they should, they don't ignore their money matters either. This is known as getting by, the apparent benefit of which is to make them susceptible to the lure of get-rich quick schemes. It's not enough that people don't become rich in these deals; more often than not, they stand to lose what is put in them. A warning buzzer should sound in your head when words like *easy, fast, no risk, secret formula,* and similar terms are used to describe a last chance to wealth. There are no *easy, fast, secret* ways to earn money without risk. How much of a secret can it be if it is offered to millions of people? Yet people are taken in by these same promises every day. Earn five hundred dollars a week in your spare time? Why only your spare time? Think of what you could earn by working full time, if it were not a hoax. Earn money with no investment or risk? Sign up for a deal like this and you will learn about investment—and a lot more about risk. Granted, more income may be needed to acquire those family wants on the postponed list. But that is no reason to throw away the money that has been accumulated on easy, fast deals that cost money. You will do better with slow and steady progress. And you will sleep better, too.

Savings

To lose the money game impressively, don't save. Then you can impress friends with this argument: why save when inflation is eating up dollars faster than they can be saved? Even though you will lose, there is some truth in this argument. To understand this, put some money in a savings account. Then come back in a year. While you are gone, the bank or savings institution will pay interest on the money. Also, during this time, the inflation monster is back there nibbling away on the dollars. When you come back in a year and withdraw the money, you will have more dollars than was first put into savings. Smile. And on the way out, pay Uncle Sam his share of the interest. You, last of the financial wizards, still have in hand more dollars than at the beginning of this little test. Unfortunately, they are worth less because they have been chewed on and otherwise maligned by inflation. If you don't believe it, go to the store. Those dollars buy fewer wants than they used to buy. Sure, you have more dollars in hand, but they may be worth only ninety cents compared to last year's dollars.

Are you better off for saving? Yes. If those dollars had been spent instead of saved, you would not have them at all, chewed on or not. True, an investment could have been made with them. But there is no guarantee that an investment won't be chewed on by the inflation monster or even that your original investment will be returned. You need some savings, regardless of inflation. Savings may not keep up with the inflation monster, but you will at least have more dollars for future wants than by not saving. While you are arguing the virtues of a favorite investment over savings, remember that the choice is more often between spending now or saving to spend later.

Investments

Admittedly, there are investments—good ones—that can do a better job of staying ahead of inflation. Why be nibbled to death when it is possible to do something about it? These days an infinite variety of investments exist from which to choose, many of them that promise to run their little legs off to stay ahead of the inflation monster. But at the race track, some things never change—most notably, the old truths that hold up day after day, no matter what new entry is in the race. Take this one: Don't invest more than you can afford to lose. But people do. Seldom do they transgress to the point of losing the house and putting their family out in the street. No, they lose in more sophisticated ways, like investing in maybe, options or commodities and pacing the floor night after night with worry over their money. Why invest this way? You are better off with the money in savings if the risk is more than can be comfortably tolerated. What advantage is there in gaining wealth at the expense of your health? Another old saying that still makes a lot of sense goes like this: Don't put all your eggs in one basket. And once again, people make the same mistake, knowing full well that their portfolio—the sum total of all their investments—should be diversified to balance the risk. Spreading the risk among different investments improves the odds in your favor. Everyone knows these old wisdoms, but some people ignore them just the same. And they lose dollars for it.

Worse, they invest in things that they know nothing about. Your brother-in-law may be making a killing in pork belly futures. Fine. He is either lucky or he knows the commodities game, or both. Even so, he can lose his shirt. If you know zilch about commodities futures, the odds of indecent exposure are worse for you. If you are not invested in the stock market, futures, options, or metals, don't automatically assume that your money belongs in them. If you know something about antique cars or real estate, investing in these allows drawing on your strengths rather than weaknesses. The only thing between you and easy street is not what someone else knows—it is making the most of your own special talents. Lean toward investments that allow you to use them.

If you don't know about an investment, learn the game or at least the basics of it, before jumping in. Brokerage houses, trading exchanges, and financial institutions are more than happy to fill your mailbox with educational material to learn the basics. Do people bother to learn? Sometimes, but more often, they hand over the money to someone else to invest for them without knowing even the fundamentals. It pays to do your own investigating. Read annual reports and other financial information. Learn all that you possibly can about a particular investment before putting money into it. The tuition for this education depends on how much is learned. The expensive school, the one people can't afford too often, is the school of hard knocks. No one is more concerned about your money than you are. Nor should they be. If you don't care enough to learn the game and seek professional advice, don't be surprised if the outcome is less than expected.

Seeking sound, professional advice is different from getting cheap advice from Louie down the street who once attended a birthday party for a stock expert's cat. Even so, you will do better listening to Louie than buying investments over the phone from strangers. And that goes double for hot tips. Anyone who claims to have a hot tip on an investment probably has a coat full of watches, so pick out a good one if you intend to throw away money this way. Even if hot tips were reliable—which they are not—by the time you hear them, they aren't very hot anymore. Buy financial products and advice from reputable firms or persons. One way or another, you pay for advice. Like most things in life, you get what you pay for.

Everyone is an expert these days. But knowing family goals can help distinguish the quality of the advice received. While everyone else is waiting to overhear hot tips on investment opportunities, you can slip quietly out of the house and head straight for the office of a reputable advisor who has been in business awhile and whose office will still be there tomorrow. Tell him your goals and ask him to match them with some investment choices. If he can't match them, exit. If he has a hot tip on the world shortage of sugar, mention the baked potatoes you left in the oven and make a graceful exit. Then find another advisor. A good one is worth the money because he can select investments that will achieve your objectives for income or growth. It's one of the nicer things he can do for you, besides returning your phone calls. What's more, he can arrange a portfolio that will provide good tax benefits in the process.

Here are a few matchmaking guidelines to check the advice that might be received:

For a good, safe investment where the money is readily accessible, invest in treasury bills or bonds, money market funds, certificates of deposit, or similar instruments designed for safety of principle, meaning you want to be certain of getting the money back—no ifs, ands, or buts.

To build a nest egg, people often choose common stocks or mutual funds that invest in stocks. Why? Because a diversified stock portfolio can grow in value faster than inflation and return sizable gains.

If you prefer interest or dividend income, government or corporate bonds, mutual funds targeted for income, treasury bills, or preferred stocks are ideal for this purpose. My father, who is retired, likes this group because his capital is generally secure and he receives steady earnings from his investments.

People looking for tax advantages find municipal bonds, real estate, or common stocks appealing. The municipal bonds are not taxed, real estate provides tremendous tax advantages, and stock held for capital gains tax treatment works fine if the stock goes up. Of course, tax laws can change overnight. At this writing, the government is thinking about eliminating some of the tax advantages in these investments. Do check with a tax advisor before investing. To fall in love with tax-advantaged investments, all you need is to pay taxes.

If you prefer higher risk in return for higher rewards, options and commodities futures afford this opportunity. Or, you can try speculating in raw land, as my friend Dave did. Maybe a developer will build a high-rise apartment building on your land, in which case you may reap sizable profits. Then again, he may wait until the next century to do it, in which case, you and Dave are feeding the alligator, as real estate people sometimes say when talking about property that consumes cash and doesn't give any money back for long periods of time, like centuries.

Nontraditional investors prefer gold, silver, rare coins, and maybe, stockpiling a year's worth of food. If you are one of them, be my guest.

Or, you can become a hard-core gambler and invest in your children's education, figuring they will pay you back when they become rich and famous.

Debt

Another enormous mistake you can make in the money game is having too much debt. With a little creative borrowing, debt can improve inflow dramatically. This allows you to obtain more wants now, not later. The only thing needed is to make certain inflow is dripping in fast enough to keep up with the payments. But too much debt is a big weight to carry. It takes away an ability to adjust to changing events. And you borrow not only from creditors, but from future choices as well. Don't mortgage your family's future to live too grandly in the present. Otherwise, next year's good times or all the wonderful things planned for the years ahead will be replaced by your own private little recession while you pay off old debts. Keep debts to a reasonable level to avoid the excess weight.

This doesn't mean that debt should be avoided entirely. Throughout our lifetimes, we use credit extensively. It is an important tool to help us win the money game, if we use it wisely. It makes sense at times to use debt to obtain some things sooner and avoid paying higher prices later on. Buying a house with the help of a mortgage is one way a lot of people make debt work for them. Or, you can use debt to cash in on the idea of using other people's money to earn more money. This is an old idea, but it still has a lot of appeal, especially when considering the use of your worst enemy's money to become rich. Does it work—this old idea of increasing earnings using other people's money?

Surprisingly, yes. Using other people's money to earn money, better known as leverage in polite circles, simply means borrowing money to enhance earnings on an investment. This is different from using debt to buy those consumer items that depreciate in value, such as a holiday cruise for two. This use of debt is for making investments that can grow in value, such as stocks or real estate—the idea being that if they grow, you stand to profit from the investment. So how do you improve earnings using other people's money?

Buy turkeys. That's what one smart young investor did. He borrowed twelve thousand dollars from his banker and bought turkeys. He reasoned that turkeys would, given a fair chance and plenty of feed, go up in value. With an eight percent loan (this was back in the old days when they loaned money for such ridiculous rates) and three thousand dollars of his own money, he bought thousands of these simple birds. Later, he sold the whole feathery lot of them for a handsome profit. He did, as they say in the turkey business, very well. After paying off his loan plus the interest and depositing his original investment back in his bank account, he pocketed three thousand dollars profit. Since three thousand dollars was the amount of his own money in this deal, he walked away with a return on his investment of roughly one hundred percent ($3,000 divided by $3,000).*

---

* Our investor made a contract with the grower to raise his turkeys for a percentage of the profits, thereby eliminating the need to invest more of his own money to feed the birds. For simplicity, no taxes were considered; though if we did, he still made out like a bandit.

Not bad for a turkey investment. The money he borrowed gave him leverage. Without it, his required investment in this deal would have been fifteen thousand dollars. Assuming he had this amount and was willing to invest it all in turkeys, his return would have dropped to about twenty percent ($3,000 divided by $15,000). Now, I've made some turkey investments where a twenty percent return would have been a blessing. Even so, when a hundred percent return can be earned, why settle for less?

If investments yield a much greater return than the cost of borrowing, you will love leverage. Leverage is kind to investors who pull off such feats. Why? Because lenders are content with a fixed return—interest—at some future date.* Once they receive their money back plus the interest, they don't care if the rest of the profits go to the investor. With leverage, the more dollars an investment earns, the more your share of the take increases over the lenders. Why are lenders so generous? Because if anything goes wrong, they still get paid. Lenders figure your money is on the line first, which is why you are going to bust your tail feathers not to lose it. You will, too. But in case there are any doubts, lenders may require collateral such as the house, the jewelry, or the silverware to make sure they get their money back.

You take most of the risk. And the risk is that an investment won't earn as expected. Instead of returning a hundred percent profit, a turkey investment might return a zero profit, or even a loss—which is what turkey investments have been known to do. When this happens, you face negative leverage—a situation similar to staring down both barrels of a double-barrel shotgun. The first barrel blows away some, if not all, of your original investment. To make matters worse, you still owe the lender. So while you stand shivering in your underwear, the second barrel takes aim at cash assets, blowing a hole in your money sack large enough to allow the lender to extract his money. It is an exciting way to lose your dollars.

---

* Interest is not as fixed as it once was. Banks and other financial institutions are sometimes reluctant to make fixed interest rate loans these days. Instead, they lend money on a floating or variable interest rate. This requires guessing what the financing costs will be. This is another risk to add to the leverage game.

Leverage is great when it works in your favor. Using debt is a smart way to increase the return on investments when earning considerably more than the cost of borrowing. But it's not wise if you pick the wrong investment and earn less than the cost of debt. While figuring the odds of earning more than the interest charges, you can do yourself a favor by not crawling out on a limb, carrying too much debt.

Taxes

Depending on how you look at it, paying taxes is one of your wants. Either you are paying to avoid jail or you consider it a duty to support the government, however wasteful it may be. It is not a duty to pay more taxes than absolutely necessary. This means that people don't win by overpaying their taxes and taking away dollars that could be used to buy other wants. This is why tax shelters have outlasted hula hoops as a national craze. But people sometimes get carried away with sheltering income from taxes. If they spent half as much time planning family goals as they spent in planning taxes, they would be better off for it. Entire industries have grown up around the idea of lowering your income taxes. Noble idea that this is, what we could all use is more attention to obtaining our family wants. Even so, tax planning is wise when we don't lose sight of goals. With this priority in place, you can benefit from sound tax planning and advice.

There was a time when tax planning was only for the wealthy. But not any more. Even if you prepare your own tax return and even if you don't have great sums of money, tax planning can be profitable. You need either to spend a great part of your life trying to understand the tax laws or see your friendly expert. You may know how to fill out the forms. But tax planning is not the same thing. During the year, there are hundreds of ways to reduce taxes. The difficult task is recognizing them in advance so that wise choices can be made. How much is your overtime worth? Maybe not as much as you think. If the extra pay forces you into a higher tax bracket, those additional earnings might be very little more than a regular pay rate when all is said and done. In this case, you get the late hours and Uncle Sam gets the bulk of the extra money. If this split doesn't thrill you, think about investing in your own little business after hours and getting the tax advantages that go with it. By working at home, you may be able to deduct part of the upkeep on a house from taxes as a business expense. Or you might deduct a portion of the operating costs on a car if it is used for business purposes. In some cases, an employer may even find it advantageous to hire your business rather than pay the overtime wages. Stranger things have happened. See a tax advisor and discover your options.

Do you have any tax-free income from sources such as municipal bonds? Or is your money sitting in savings while you pay tax on the interest? It's amazing how many of us pass up these opportunities for cutting taxes when we only need to transfer some money out of savings and buy a good-quality stock or bond. Instead, most of us skip over these items on our tax form and figure that they apply to someone else, like scientists in Antarctica. If the government allows two hundred dollars dividend income each year tax-free, why not take advantage of this opportunity? If the high cost of Junior's college education has you in a state of shock, why not see a tax advisor for possible ways to help finance the cost with tax advantages? Since you are in a little partnership with Uncle Sam and others who tax income, you can cut their share of the take. This leaves more money for your family. And tax planning, if it is done early can pay off handsomely. But don't wait until two days before the end of the year. By then, you won't have many options.

Buy The Bargains

To acquire additional wants, you can earn more, share less with your partners, or pay less for those things on the wish list. There are some people—and we all know a few of them—who somehow manage to get by on less money and still have more than the rest of us. How they manage this feat may be a mystery, but it is a good bet that one of their secrets is *buying the bargains.* Invariably, these people know what they want. What's more, they know how much to pay for it. It's easy to assume that the stated price is the best price available. But by assuming this, you waste dollars that could be going toward other goals. Although everyone would like you to think differently, the price is almost always negotiable. Each of us has a built-in price meter. When we buy wisely, the meter registers satisfaction from knowing that a good buy has been made. When we pay too much, the meter registers a definite irritation. Unfortunately, we forget to turn on the meter before buying. True, it has an automatic switch. But this feature only works after you have paid the money.

Quick Ways To Lose

Of all the graceful ways to lose the money game, family fights over money matters is the most inept way to do it. If you are going to lose, do it in style. Let them repossess your Cadillac. Or take a last cruise around the world on your good looks and credit cards. But don't spend energy fighting over money. As a family, you are in this money game together for better or worse. It is impossible to win when you are divided and constantly bickering over money matters. Moreover, fighting destroys the teamwork needed to obtain family wants.

If there is a universal mistake that most of us make, it is not having a plan. Managing money without a plan gives you all the perspective of a nearsighted rhino in handling family finances. Do you have too much debt? Are you saving those dollars without a purpose in mind? The trouble is that you are so close to the trees—daily decisions on money matters—that the view of the forest is obscured. Without seeing the big picture of finances, it is difficult to tell the direction that your family is headed. In the end, the decisions made each day are the ones that finally determine the outcome. But it takes a plan to steer a straight course to your family's wants.

Playing To Win

Obviously, the way to win the money game is to do the opposite of all those things that can make us lose. You don't need get-rich-quick schemes, too much debt, or investments where the risk is too great for the potential reward. Nor do you need to bury your head in the sand and figure that family finances will take care of themselves. Winning requires facing up to a money past and looking for ways to improve spending habits. It also requires working together as a family to decide on the things that are desired, the ones that are most important, and the ones that must be temporarily delayed, but that will be picked up later. You can win by saving or investing for goals in the distant future to enjoy your retirement years. You can win by using debt wisely to improve a return on an investment. But most of all, you can win by making a plan to reach family goals. With a plan and a method to follow, you have the advantage.

Besides these obvious actions, how you approach the challenge makes all the difference in the world. This is a fun game, or it should be. If you don't enjoy your life along the way, you will lose. Remember, Aunt Hilda was partly right: how the game is played *does* count. By playing the game in a way that everyone in your family enjoys, you can win. Whether rich, poor, or in-between, we all share one thing in common: time. Don't waste this precious commodity by failing to enjoy your life because of money matters. Even if you make it to the top with your finances and incur misery in the process, you will lose the game.

Winning means getting your family's wants. But it doesn't mean getting them all at once. Take away the fun of winning, of making progress and getting ahead, and those wants won't mean nearly as much. It's the small victories we savor—the ones we remember and the ones that fill our scrapbooks. Looking back, it's not the numbers. It's the kids we got through school, the family reunion that brought us all together again, or the times we shared with others. Winning is your daughter's piano recital where those endless lessons and practice sessions finally paid off. Winning is the satisfaction received from helping someone when they needed your help most. Even the last mortgage payment—the one that was framed and hung on the wall— is what winning is all about.

Some things in life cost very little, yet their value is so great that nothing else compares to them. What is the value of a father's carefully baited fish hook to show a son how to catch his first fish? Or, how much is the moment worth when a mother sees a reflection of her own childhood as she helps a daughter sew her first dress? Don't throw away these special times together with your family. Nothing can replace them. No amount of money buys the time when you do something silly to make your spouse laugh and win each other's hearts all over again. Once allowed to go by, these occasions can never be replaced. It's easy to be caught up in finances and lose sight of the reason for playing the money game. Capture those priceless family wants. Plan money matters in a way that leaves room for them in your life ahead. These goals are inexpensive, unless they are traded away for too many business meetings or time spent pursuing other things that pale in comparison. Then, their price is too high.

Sometimes we look at our past through rose-colored glasses, remembering things not as they were, but as we wished them to be. Each of us possesses this talent, yet we often look at our future in a completely different way, expecting the worst of things to come. How much better it is to see the future in the same way that we often look at the past. Granted, we risk disappointment at times, but by viewing our future through rose-colored glasses, we can make some of our great expectations become reality, when they are accompanied by a plan to get them.

But looking ahead is not easy. In this direction, we tend to get nearsighted—the budgeted amount we will overspend or tomorrow's bills that we must pay. Still, we can improve our vision with some practice and a plan. And with our focus well ahead of the present, we keep the present in perspective and make the most of it.

Strange as it may seem, too many of us don't know why we play the money game—to get our family's wants. The ways to win are as varied as the people who play. But over time, there are no second–place finishes or honorable mentions in the money game. Either your family wins or they don't. Naturally, I wish you luck. But with a good plan, you won't need it.